Vahan Janjigian is chief investment strategist at Forbes. *He is coauthor of the* Forbes Stock Market Course, *editor of the* Forbes Growth Investor *and* Special Situation Survey *investment newsletters, and a frequent contributor to* Forbes *and* Forbes.com. *He also sits on the investment committee of Hillview Capital Advisors, LLC. He lives in Rye Brook, New York.*

Praise for Even Buffett Isn't Perfect

"Vahan Janjigian delineates a cornucopia of little nuggets about Mr. Buffett that every Buffettphile will want, and aspects basic to investing that everyone, novice or top-tier pro, should know."

> —Ken Fisher, founder and CEO, Fisher Investments;
> author of *The Only Three Questions That Count*;
> and *Forbes*'s "Portfolio Strategy" columnist

"Vahan Janjigian is the guru that other gurus turn to when they want advice. By taking the novel approach of examining not only what Buffett does right but what, occasionally, he has done wrong, Even Buffett Isn't Perfect *provides both an invaluable education about successful investment strategies and deep insight into the mind and tactics of the one investor whose secrets everyone wants to know."*

> —Vartan Gregorian, president, Carnegie Corporation of
> New York

"Anyone who thinks he understands Warren Buffett's approach to investing should read this book. Marrying the wisdom of the grandmaster with the latest research on investment strategy, Vahan debunks more than a few myths and delivers a brand-new look at the creative thinking that has made Buffett the 'world's greatest value investor.'"

> —Ian Bremmer, president, Eurasia Group and author of
> *The J Curve*

"Janjigian's closely reasoned new study of Warren Buffett, warts and all, will be mined by prospective emulators everywhere stocks are traded. Among other features, the several myths of Buffett's practice are matched against performance realities."

—Robert H. Stovall, Sr., managing director and strategist, Wood Asset Management, Inc.

"In 2006, Warren shared with Bill the Buffett fortune. Now, Vahan shares with us the Buffett wisdom."

—Sam Stovall, chief investment strategist, Standard & Poor's

"Vahan Janjigian's insights and observations about Warren Buffett show that hard work, diligence, and patience usually result in investment success—but a little luck helps also. However, Janjigian points out that Buffett is far less than perfect with regard to taxes and taxation."

—Leon Charney, host and moderator, *The Leon Charney Report*

"This is one of the best Buffett books to come along in years. Vahan's thoughtful and provoking presentation is a must-have book for any investor who wants to build on the very best of Warren Buffett."

—Liz Ann Sonders, chief investment strategist, Charles Schwab & Co., Inc.

Even Buffett Isn't Perfect

What You Can—and Can't—Learn from
the World's Greatest Investor

Vahan Janjigian

Portfolio

PORTFOLIO

Published by the Penguin Group

Penguin Group (USA) Inc., 375 Hudson Street, New York, New York 10014, U.S.A.
Penguin Group (Canada), 90 Eglinton Avenue East, Suite 700, Toronto, Ontario,
Canada M4P 2Y3 (a division of Pearson Penguin Canada Inc.)
Penguin Books Ltd, 80 Strand, London WC2R 0RL, England
Penguin Ireland, 25 St Stephen's Green, Dublin 2, Ireland (a division of Penguin Books Ltd)
Penguin Group (Australia), 250 Camberwell Road, Camberwell, Victoria 3124, Australia
(a division of Pearson Australia Group Pty Ltd)
Penguin Books India Pvt Ltd, 11 Community Centre, Panchsheel Park,
New Delhi – 110 017, India
Penguin Group (NZ), 67 Apollo Drive, Rosedale, North Shore 0632, New Zealand
(a division of Pearson New Zealand Ltd)
Penguin Books (South Africa) (Pty) Ltd, 24 Sturdee Avenue, Rosebank,
Johannesburg 2196, South Africa

Penguin Books Ltd, Registered Offices:
80 Strand, London WC2R 0RL, England

First published in the United States of America by Portfolio,
a member of Penguin Group (USA) Inc. 2008
This paperback edition published 2009

3   5   7   9   10   8   6   4   2

PUBLISHER'S NOTE: This publication is designed to provide accurate and authoritative information
in regard to the subject matter covered. It is sold with the understanding that the publisher is
not engaged in rendering legal, accounting, or other professional services. If you require legal
advice or other expert assistance, you should seek the services of a competent professional.

THE LIBRARY OF CONGRESS HAS CATALOGED THE HARDCOVER EDITION AS FOLLOWS:
Janjigian, Vahan.
Even Buffett isn't perfect : what you can—and can't—learn from
the world's greatest investor / Vahan Janjigian.
p.   cm.
Includes bibliographical references and index.
ISBN 978-1-59184-196-8 (hc.)
ISBN 978-1-59184-270-5 (pbk.)
1. Investments.   2. Stocks.   3. Buffett, Warren.   I. Title.
HG4521.J286   2008
332.6—dc22   2007042692

Printed in the United States of America

Dedicated to

Ross Abdallah Alameddine
Christopher James Bishop
Brian Roy Bluhm
Ryan Christopher Clark
Austin Michelle Cloyd
Jocelyne Couture-Nowak
Kevin P. Granata
Matthew Gregory Gwaltney
Caitlin Millar Hammaren
Jeremy Michael Herbstritt
Rachael Elizabeth Hill
Emily Jane Hilscher
Jarrett Lee Lane
Matthew Joseph La Porte
Henry J. Lee
Liviu Librescu
G. V. Loganathan

Partahi Mamora Halomoan
    Lumbantoruan
Lauren Ashley McCain
Daniel Patrick O'Neil
Juan Ramon Ortiz-Ortiz
Minal Hiralal Panchal
Daniel Alejandro Perez
Erin Nicole Peterson
Michael Steven Pohle, Jr.
Julia Kathleen Pryde
Mary Karen Read
Reema Joseph Samaha
Waleed Mohamed Shaalan
Leslie Geraldine Sherman
Maxine Shelly Turner
Nicole Regina White

Contents

Foreword

Vahan Janjigian is particularly well qualified to write about Warren Buffett. While the Sage of Omaha has been the subject of a number of books, this one is unique. It is neither a love letter nor a put-down. Vahan is an excellent stock picker—he oversees the *Forbes Special Situation Survey* and the *Forbes Growth Investor* newsletter, and his performance has been excellent. Subscribers have benefited from Vahan's acutely analytical, nonemotional methods. Vahan thus has the insight to truly appreciate how unique Warren Buffett's own extraordinary performance at Berkshire Hathaway has been. He carefully, patiently explains Buffett's disciplined and farsighted approach and how it has evolved as Berkshire Hathaway's assets have grown.

But this isn't just an informed analysis of the Buffett phenomenon—Vahan skillfully uses the man's insights and successes to teach you things you need to know to do well consistently in the market. And Vahan carefully analyzes other investment strategies—there is more than one way to do well on Wall Street.

The trouble with most investors is that they ricochet from one approach to another. Few have Buffett's ability to stay with stocks for years on end. And few have the ability to constantly apply the various strategies Vahan examines here. But if you are willing to put your emotions on the shelf, this book will be a treasure trove of insights.

No investor always gets it right. Human beings are incapable of doing that. Buffett himself has a hard time selling stocks he has bought. He often rides his winners too long. But by having a sound, consistent approach—even if modified over time—Buffett has done fantastically well.

Luckily, you don't have to be Buffett to get excellent stock market returns. The miracle of compounding means that any careful investor can achieve long-term real success.

What makes this book especially valuable is that Vahan Janjigian does not wear blinders, wisely recognizing that investing does not take place in a vacuum. His chapter on taxes is a must-read for everyone, especially politicos. Amazingly, a genius like Buffett is shortsighted in this critical area. When Arnold Schwarzenegger decided to run for governor of California, Buffett advised him to advocate an increase in the property taxes, something that would have kept Arnold on a Hollywood movie lot rather than moving him into the governor's mansion.

Like many in Washington, Buffett thinks the "rich" should face higher income tax rates. He is also a full-throated advocate of high death taxes.

Buffett believes that we live in a great country and that those lucky enough to do well in it should pay a greater proportion of their income in taxes. The irony here is that if Buffett's advice was followed, the economy would perform poorly and the value of Buffett's investments would take a hard hit. Just look at the miserable performance of equities and the economy during the high-tax 1970s.

What the Sage and too many others don't recognize is that taxes are a price and a burden and not just a means of raising revenue for the government. A tax on income is the price you pay for working; a tax on profits is the burden you bear for being successful; and the tax you pay on capital gains is the price you pay for taking risks that work out. The principle is basic: If you lessen the burden on positive things such as productive work, risk taking, and success, they will occur more often. Raise the price and the opposite will happen. As Janjigian points out, the top 1 percent of income earners in America earn 21 percent of the income—and pay 39 percent of federal income taxes.

Buffett is equally obtuse on the subject of death taxes. He favors retaining them, believing that the government should take a big chunk of your wealth. Otherwise, your heirs might get it and the windfall could undermine their character and tempt them to lead lives of irresponsible indulgence. Perversely, though, death taxes punish capital creation and frugality. What's the point of accumulating an estate if a big chunk of it will simply fall into the hands of the government? As Vahan notes: "Wealth is what is left over *after* taxes have been paid." Our Founders might have put the issue this way: "No taxation without respiration."

The death tax has a peculiar impact that Buffett and other supporters overlook. When rates are high the very wealthy find ways to avoid them. Buffett's own death tax liability will be low since he is giving away most of his money to the Bill & Melinda Gates Foundation. The truly rich set up elaborate trusts and other stratagems to keep their capital intact, and that usually means the heirs can't get their hands on it directly. The wealth is thus preserved. Without a death tax most assets would pass directly into the hands of children and grandchildren, most of whom don't have the entrepreneurial instinct; therefore, the money would be quickly recycled. That's human nature. Look, for instance, at the *Forbes* 400 list of America's richest. Today it contains not one du Pont and only one Rockefeller; both families twenty-five years ago controlled formidable fortunes.

Believers in high taxes studiously ignore history. The big Reagan income tax rate cuts of 1981 and 1986 turned a stagnant economy into the world's most dynamic. The U.S. share of global GDP went up sharply, as did the share of America's equity of the world's total equity value. Because Reagan wanted to win the cold war, thereby rebuilding our dilapidated military, and because Congress was—as usual—addicted to domestic spending, federal outlays mushroomed and the national debt went up $1.7 trillion. What skeptics refuse to recognize is that the wealth of the nation during that period went up $17 trillion. There is not a CEO around who wouldn't gladly exchange $1 of debt for $10 of equity.

The Clinton tax increase of 1993 sharply slowed the growth of the U.S. economy and contributed to the Democratic rout in the 1994 congressional elections. With the Republicans in charge of Congress, taxophile President Clinton was cornered. His wife's socialized medicine scheme went down in flames. Spending was restrained. And, most important, there were positive tax moves: the capital gains levy was cut almost 29 percent. Capital gains taxes on homeowners' primary residences were virtually eliminated and a moratorium on Internet taxation passed into law, which contributed enormously to its rapid development. The Bush tax cuts of 2003—the capital gains tax was cut again, the personal dividend tax was slashed by more than 60 percent, personal income tax rates were reduced, and incentives for business to invest were put in place—turned the U.S. economy from only 1 percent real growth to a 3 to 4 percent growth rate. Between 2003 and 2007 the growth of the U.S. economy alone exceeded the entire size of the Chinese economy. And guess what? Equities boomed, almost doubling from their lows of late 2002.

Vahan points out another area where Buffett is shortsighted: earnings guidance. Most large publicly held companies give security analysts ranges of what they think earnings will be for each quarter. If companies miss the range on the down side—even if by only a penny a share—their stocks often get clobbered. Buffett feels this kind of guidance contributes to stock market volatility and forces management to be too short-term oriented. He has "persuaded" companies where he has large stakes, such as Coca-Cola and The Washington Post Company, not to provide guidance.

Vahan gives a very persuasive, sophisticated rebuttal. Investors will make estimates anyway. Moreover, management should be providing *more* information to investors rather than less. As to volatility, studies have shown that companies that don't provide guidance very often can be as whipsawed as those that do. More important, companies that don't provide guidance will have a smaller market cap than those that do. In other words, companies that give earnings estimates will generally have higher stock prices than those that don't.

So what we have here is an unusual book. It focuses on the most successful investor in modern times. But it also gives readers an array of insights and strategies for investing in the market. And finally, its prescriptions in the areas of taxation and corporate transparency would create an environment where equity values would expand.

In essence, you are getting three books in one, which makes this "asset" an undervalued one!

Steve Forbes
CEO and Chairman, Forbes Inc.
Editor in Chief, *Forbes* Magazine

Introduction

On June 26, 2006, America's then second-richest man announced that he was giving most of his money to America's richest man. Seated next to Bill and Melinda Gates at the New York Public Library, Warren Buffett made public his plan to donate 10 million shares of Berkshire Hathaway Class B common stock, worth about $31 billion at the time, to the Bill & Melinda Gates Foundation. He also pledged an additional 2 million shares, or $6.3 billion, to foundations run by his three children, including one named for his deceased wife. In one fell swoop, the man who achieved fame by building one of the greatest fortunes the world has ever seen ensured that he would be remembered just as much for giving almost all of it away.

Buffett's fortune is indeed vast. He created it by investing. In fact, Buffett is arguably the greatest investor of all time. Without a doubt, he certainly has one of the best long-term track records in the business. Because he heads Berkshire Hathaway, a publicly traded company, his investment decisions are fully disclosed and easily monitored. Buffett took control of Berkshire in the 1960s and eventually transformed it from a textile company into an investment company. During his reign as CEO, he made a fortune for himself and his shareholders.

Buffett's thinking is sometimes unconventional. Most investors, for example, like to see the prices of the stocks they purchase rise quickly. Not Buffett. He says the only time you should want stock prices to go up is when you are ready to sell. Because Buffett is a long-term investor, he does not want to see prices rise right away. In fact, if he really likes a stock, he is happier if the price falls so he can buy more shares at a lower price and really reduce his cost basis. This way, when prices finally recover, he ends up sitting on huge gains. This kind of thinking has resulted in Berkshire's unrealized capital gains of $8.5 billion on American Express, $8 billion on Coca-Cola, $5.5 billion on Procter & Gamble, and $4 billion on Wells Fargo. Some stocks in Berkshire's portfolio have also produced huge percentage returns. Its gain on The Washington Post Company alone comes out to 11,600 percent!

One of Buffett's greatest attributes is that he knows his limitations. For example, he knows he can't be an expert in every industry. But insurance is one industry he understands very well. He developed a knack for assessing risk. And he figured out how to invest insurance premiums at a rate high enough to pay future claims and have plenty left over for shareholders.

Buffett has always followed a disciplined investment approach. He is well known for avoiding "hot" investment styles and strategies that eventually turned out to be nothing but passing fads. For example, the U.S. stock markets were booming during the mid- to late 1990s, driven largely by technology stocks. Buffett famously eschewed the very same stocks that were pushing the market indexes ever higher. He did not even buy Microsoft, even though the company was led by his good friend Bill Gates.

Buffett was widely criticized for missing out on that tech-led rally, but he pays little attention to critics. Nor do his Berkshire shareholders. They understood his long-term approach and they were confident that under Buffett's direction they would be pleased with their returns.

Buffett sticks with what he knows best. He likes companies that operate in simple businesses he can understand. He does not understand how to value software and semiconductors. He thinks their cash flows are too difficult to project with any degree of certainty. However, he knows a great deal about valuing beverages, razor blades, and banks. He also likes companies that have honest and talented managers. And most of all, he wants to buy companies for less than their intrinsic value, and hold on to them for a very long time. This is a strategy that has proved tremendously rewarding to him and his Berkshire Hathaway shareholders for more than four decades.

Back in the 1990s, however, there were many investors who thought Buffett had lost his touch. They did not care how successful he had been over the long term. They were convinced he was now missing the boat. At that time, many investors had come to believe we had entered a new age. In fact, pundits called it the "new economy." They said the old rules no longer applied. These investors did not hesitate to snap up stocks that were selling for multiples they would have labeled ridiculously high just a short time earlier.

Perhaps this kind of thinking is best illustrated by a letter sent to the *Forbes Special Situation Survey* by one of its subscribers. It was written in early 2000, at the tail end of what became known as the dot-com bubble, in response to a stock recommendation—the stock of a company that was part of what at the time was referred to as the "old economy." There was nothing high-tech about this stock. In fact, it was the kind of stock that Buffett himself might have favored. But the subscriber wrote, "Do you really expect me to buy a stock that might go up only about 40% in two years? I'm 80 years old. I don't have forever to make some money!"

The letter sounds like a joke, but the writer was stone-cold serious. Her words clearly attest to the unreasonable and unsustainable level investors' expectations had reached in those heady days. It is easy to look back now and say investors should have known better. Unfortunately, many investors allowed themselves to get caught up in the "madness of the crowd." Buffett never falls into this trap. He is the master of cool. He always thinks rationally and methodically. Thinking and investing the Buffett way can be particularly profitable when everyone else is giving in to their emotions and the madness of the day.

According to the stock market research firm Ibbotson Associates, the arithmetic average long-term total rate of return (i.e., including dividends) for large-cap stocks is about 12 percent per year. For small-cap stocks the figure is better—about 17 percent per year.[1]

Yet in the late 1990s, investors wanted much more. They kept hearing about Internet stocks with funny names that seemed to double or triple in price every few months. In fact, many companies added ".com" to the end of their name, convinced that it would attract more interest. Survey after survey indicated that investors thought it was quite reasonable to earn 20 percent or more each and every year in the stock market. They were not interested in buying stocks that might generate more modest rates of return—even if those returns were somewhat better than the historical averages. And they certainly were not interested in value stocks.

Buffett, however, knew better. He is one of the most astute students of the financial markets, and has been for decades. He pays attention to long-term trends, and he knew that rational investing had given in to mass euphoria (or "irrational exuberance," as former Fed chairman Alan Greenspan put it).

Buffett was intimately familiar with the Ibbotson research. He knew that well-above-average returns can't continue indefinitely. Markets always fall following a frothy period of unprecedented returns. Like Buffett, other rational investors were derided in the press for their conservative views in the late 1990s. David Dreman, for example, cautioned investors in his *Forbes* column that stocks had become much too expensive. One reader called him a dinosaur who did not understand that things were different this time.

Of course, events eventually proved the Buffetts and Dremans of this world right. But in those inebriating dot-com days, investors had become extremely greedy. They were not going to be satisfied with so-called reasonable rates of return. They wanted to make a lot of money, and they wanted to make it quickly. And because the markets were rising and some of their own stocks were going through the roof, they all became convinced that they, too, were investment experts. Some even thought they were smarter than Buffett. Good sense and patience went out the window, and many of those investors eventually went broke. Buffett, on the other hand, is richer than ever.

Nonetheless, the letter writer made an interesting point. Warren Buffett, who has a solid reputation of being a long-term investor, does not think favorably of those who prefer to make a quick buck through short-term trading. Buffett has said his favorite holding period is forever. But our eighty-year-old letter writer did not give a hoot about the long term. She clearly had a much shorter investment horizon in mind.

Unfortunately, she was looking to make some fast money just as the major stock market indexes were about to hit multiyear highs and begin a prolonged and painful decline. One can only hope she did not pour her life savings into one of those Internet or technology stocks that eventually collapsed to less than a dollar per share. Her letter made it perfectly clear that she knew exactly what she was looking for. She wanted big gains and she wanted them fast. However, she probably did not appreciate or understand the risks involved with that kind of investment strategy. Perhaps she did not even care about risk. After all, as she pointedly suggested in her letter, she was getting old and felt she could no longer afford the luxury of being patient. The Dow Jones Industrial Average and the S&P 500 took about seven years to get back to their 2000 highs. During that same time, the NASDAQ Composite Index managed to recover only about one half of its losses.

Among the many things you will learn in this book is that Warren Buffett often embraces market sell-offs. After all, a sell-off is like a fire sale at a retail store. If you have your eye on an expensive pair of shoes, would you not be more inclined to buy them when they go on sale? Similarly, if you like a stock at $50 per share, should you not like it even more at $40? Of course, shoes and stocks are not exactly the same. A pair of shoes does not change in the slightest simply because its price is reduced. But a stock's price reflects expectations about future cash flows. If the price falls, it means that investors as a whole have become less optimistic about those cash flows. They have lowered their expectations about the company's prospects.

Unlike shoe sales, stock market sell-offs can scare the pants off ordinary investors. It requires a certain amount of intestinal fortitude to be willing to jump in and buy stocks when everyone else is selling them. The risk, of course, is that you might buy too soon. Just because a stock has fallen 20 percent, there is no guarantee that it will not fall another 20 percent. One of Wall Street's more colorful adages is "Don't catch a falling knife." However, chances are that the stock of a good company will eventually recover. No one knows for sure when the recovery will occur. Indeed, it may take many years. But if you are a patient investor with a long-term outlook, you don't mind waiting. You might even use that time to load up on more shares at the lower price. Buffett, of course, is the master of long-term investing. Buffett is proof positive that exercising patience can be an incredibly profitable way to invest.

Despite Buffett's tremendous success, you will also learn that Buffett's way is not the only way to make good profits in the stock market. In fact, in some situations it is definitely not the best way. Indeed, there are many ways to invest. Some are clearly irresponsible. For example, if you went to the racetrack and put a lot of money on one horse, you would certainly not be investing. To make yourself feel better, you might call it entertainment. However, if you have any sense, you realize that it is really gambling. Likewise, putting a large sum of money on one stock is not investing either. Like betting on a horse, betting on one stock is simply gambling. At the other extreme, you can play it safe by spreading your money across a large number of stocks. This strategy, known as diversification, is one embraced by most investment professionals. However, if you diversify too much, you cannot hope to do any better than the market as a whole.

There is also a question of time. Like Buffett, you can follow a buy-and-hold strategy, investing for the very long term. Alternatively, you can follow a market-timing strategy, investing with a shorter horizon in mind. While short-term investing can be profitable, it requires a completely different mind-set. We will take a look at some of the academic research, which demonstrates that less patient investors who want to focus on shorter-term returns should favor strategies that stress growth and momentum.

We will also look at research that demonstrates that value stocks beat growth stocks over the long term. Buying a broadly diversified portfolio of value stocks and holding them for the long term is a rather safe, and perhaps boring, way to invest. But it is also a profitable strategy. On the other hand, taking concentrated positions in a much smaller number of stocks, whether it is for the short term or the long term, can be significantly more exciting. But it also involves considerably more risk.

Buffett, who has the patience of a saint, is the master of long-term investing. His personality is well suited to this kind of strategy. Yet, as you will learn in the pages ahead, even Buffett has engaged in his share of relatively short-term trades. Indeed, one valuable lesson to be learned from this book is that Buffett's investment strategies cannot be so easily pigeonholed. They have evolved over time. For example, in the beginning of his career, he showed a preference for taking large positions in a small number of companies. Although he still leans toward this concentrated approach, in recent years diversification has emerged to play a much bigger role in Buffett's style of investing.

To be a successful investor, you must be an educated investor, and the best place to start is by examining Buffett's strategies. This book will teach you the pluses and minuses of those strategies, when they work best and when they don't. It will teach you that diversification, one of the most important concepts in modern finance, not only helps you reduce investment risk; it also limits your potential gains. You will see how Buffett's views on diversification have evolved over time.

This book will teach you to understand and appreciate the difference between a value stock and an undervalued stock. This is critical to understanding how Buffett invests. The book will also teach you to know when you should tilt your portfolio toward value stocks and when you should favor growth stocks. It will even teach you about one decidedly non-Buffett strategy, momentum investing, and how you can use it to your advantage.

You will also learn in the pages ahead that no one is perfect—not even Warren Buffett. As hard as it may be to believe, even Buffett has made some mistakes. When it comes to investing, mistakes can be costly indeed. But you can learn quite a lot from your mistakes. Naturally, people prefer to forget their mistakes because they bring painful memories. Investors, however, should embrace their mistakes. When you make a mistake, as you inevitably will, do not try to purge it from your mind. Instead, burn it into your memory so you will never forget it. That way you will be sure to learn something useful, and you will be more likely to avoid getting into the rut of repeating the same mistake over and over again. Failure is often the greatest teacher, but only if you allow yourself to be taught.

Fortunately for his shareholders, Buffett's mistakes have been very few and far between. Yet when it comes to mistakes, there is one important characteristic that sets Buffett apart from so many other investors. He has demonstrated an incredible knack for turning what appear to be obvious mistakes into eventual successes. Indeed, this is one reason why Buffett is arguably the most successful—and wealthiest—investor of all time.

Speaking of wealth, each year *Forbes* magazine publishes a list of the 400 Richest Americans. It also publishes a list of the World's Billionaires. Year after year, Warren Buffett's name appears near the very top of both lists. You will learn from this book that, like most of the megarich, Buffett's fortune is tied primarily to just one company. In Buffett's case that company is Berkshire Hathaway, where he serves as both CEO and chairman of the board. However, Berkshire is a unique company.

Unlike most other companies that manufacture a core set of products or provide a specific set of services, Berkshire is more like an investment company. While it is true that Berkshire's revenues and profits are heavily dependent on the insurance industry, Berkshire's real business is to invest in other businesses. This business plan makes Berkshire somewhat like a mutual fund, and it makes Buffett somewhat like a mutual fund manager. It also makes Buffett one of the few multibillionaires who got rich primarily from investing rather than from actually starting and running an individual company focused on a specific business. Much of Berkshire's success is due to Buffett's ability to use the float from its insurance businesses to finance the purchase of other profitable companies. Indeed, this is largely why Buffett is called a great investor rather than simply a great entrepreneur.

Since there are dozens of books already written about Warren Buffett and Berkshire Hathaway, it is fair to ask why we need another. While many prior books discuss and analyze Buffett's investment strategies, most appear to be little more than love letters to a great man. While Buffett certainly deserves all the praise heaped upon him, most books written about Buffett lack objectivity. They fail to point out the flaws in his investment approach. Even when they carefully analyze Buffett's favored investment tactics, they sometimes fail to explain what it is that Buffett does that other investors can also hope to replicate. Perhaps more important, they often fail to explain what Buffett does that other investors cannot realistically hope to replicate themselves.

Furthermore, prior writers simply overlook the many issues

Buffett advocates that do not serve the best interests of investors. For example, as you will learn in the pages ahead, Buffett believes corporations should stop giving investors quarterly earnings guidance. In other words, in an age when regulators are trying to encourage corporations to increase transparency and disclose more information, Buffett is in favor of a policy that will result in corporations providing less—not more—information. Of course, as usual, his intentions are good. But as you will see, the consequences of a no-guidance policy are not good for investors.

Buffett also favors higher taxes on the so-called rich. He likes the estate tax even though he will largely avoid it himself by donating his wealth to a foundation. He opposed efforts to cut income tax rates even though the evidence suggests that lower rates spur the economy and reduce unemployment by encouraging investment and reducing the cost of capital. The evidence also shows that lower tax rates result in higher tax revenues for the government. When advising Arnold Schwarzenegger in his bid to become governor of California, Buffett recommended an increase in property taxes. Interestingly, you will also learn that Buffett admits that his reluctance to sell certain businesses at any price ends up hurting Berkshire's financial performance.

Indeed, there are plenty of myths about Warren Buffett. This book will attempt to distinguish myth from reality. For example, as mentioned earlier, many investors are convinced that Buffett despises investment strategies that favor diversification over concentration. Buffett himself has spoken disparagingly about diversification. However, you will see that in reality Buffett believes most investors should hold extensively diversified portfolios. Even Berkshire is much more diversified today than it has ever been in its long and glorious past.

Furthermore, many investors are convinced that Buffett buys

only cheap stocks, meaning stocks that have low price multiples such as low price-to-earnings ratios, which we will cover in greater depth in the chapters ahead. The reality, however, is more complicated. In fact, Buffett does not pay much attention to price multiples. Instead, like all well-trained financial analysts, he estimates future cash flows and discounts them back to the present to calculate something known as intrinsic value. He prefers to buy companies that he can get for less than intrinsic value. In other words, he likes to buy stocks cheap, not cheap stocks. This may sound like a subtle difference, but it is an important distinction you will learn about in the pages ahead.

You will also learn that, contrary to popular opinion, Buffett does not oppose the use of employee stock options. This will no doubt come as a surprise to many readers since Buffett has been a vocal critic—and rightly so—of excessive executive compensation. Buffett was even at the forefront of efforts to petition regulators to require the expensing of stock options on the financial statements. The reality, however, is that Buffett believes stock options are a perfectly appropriate tool for rewarding corporate executives—just as long as they are properly structured.

You will learn that Buffett's reputation as a shareholder rights advocate may be somewhat misplaced. Although he is one of the most ethical CEOs in America and one who clearly despises executives who enrich themselves at the expense of their shareholders, you will find out that Berkshire Hathaway had a rather dismal record of corporate governance until it was forced by the New York Stock Exchange to be more open and transparent.

A track coach once told one of his top runners, "If you want to be a faster runner, you have to train with runners who are faster than you." Similarly, if you want to be a better investor, it helps to learn from the best. They do not come much better than Warren Buffett. The bad news is that you can't simply show up at his office in Omaha and announce that you are ready to learn. The good news is that by studying his techniques, you can learn quite a lot about investing and you can make yourself a much better investor.

By studying Buffett you can learn what works and what does not work in most circumstances. By learning everything you can about Buffett's strategies, you will ensure that you have the information you need to maximize the probability of success no matter what your investment horizon. You will also develop an understanding of and appreciation for the risks involved in the various kinds of investment strategies that are available to you. And you will make yourself a more realistic investor. After all, when it comes to buying stocks, there is no such thing as a sure thing. However, over many decades of study, researchers have figured out which investment strategies work best over different investment horizons. By studying Buffett and being aware of what the research shows, you will make sure that the odds of investment success are always in your favor.

1

The *New* Diversified Buffett?

The strategy we've adopted precludes our following standard diversification dogma.

—Warren Buffett, 1993

Maybe more than 99 percent of people who invest should extensively diversify.

—Warren Buffett, 1998

These certainly seem like contradictory statements. Where exactly does Warren Buffett stand on diversification? Is he for it or is he against it? Does he follow his own advice, or is the answer far more complicated than a simple yes or no?

No doubt every investor has been told at one time or another, "Don't put all your eggs in one basket." Diversification is one of the most fundamental rules of modern portfolio theory. It is taught to finance students in universities all around the world. It is beaten into their heads in every finance course they take, from corporate finance to portfolio theory. Even the professionals are on board. Investment advisers would consider it completely irresponsible to concentrate a client's portfolio.

Finance students and investment professionals are not only

taught to diversify within asset classes, they are also taught to diversify across asset classes. This cross-asset diversification is commonly referred to as *asset allocation*. There are all kinds of asset classes. Among other things, they include stocks, bonds, real estate, and cash. The idea is that investors should not only buy different kinds of stocks; they should also buy different kinds of bonds, real estate, and other assets. In addition, they should hold some cash. Modern portfolio theory says the more varied your portfolio, the better.

Yet diversification is one rule to which Warren Buffett does not fully subscribe. To the contrary, his investment strategy has primarily been characterized as one of portfolio concentration—at least for most of his long career. Yet in more recent periods, Berkshire Hathaway, the company that Buffett and his partner Charlie Munger have been running for decades, is more diversified than it has ever been. Does this reveal a new side to Buffett's investing style? More than a decade ago, he was deriding the so-called investment experts and anyone else who recommended broad portfolio diversification. Here is what he had to say about diversification in his 1993 letter to shareholders:

> The strategy we've adopted precludes our following standard diversification dogma. Many pundits would therefore say the strategy must be riskier than that employed by more conventional investors. We disagree. We believe that a policy of portfolio concentration may well decrease risk if it raises, as it should, both the intensity with which an investor thinks about a business and the comfort-level he must feel with its economic characteristics before buying into it. In stating

this opinion, we define risk, using dictionary terms, as "the possibility of loss or injury."[1]

Perhaps to make sure there was absolutely no ambiguity in their views, Charlie Munger stated things a little more clearly. In 1996, *Barron's* quoted him as saying that modern portfolio theory is "a type of dementia I can't even classify."[2] Despite their tremendous success, if Buffett and Munger were finance professors, chances are their careers would have ended long ago.

Despite his earlier comments and his reputation for concentrating his investments, we should not conclude that Buffett has absolutely no regard for the principles of diversification and asset allocation. There is extensive evidence that he does. However, he thinks that finance theory goes much too far on this score.

Berkshire currently owns more than seventy subsidiary companies and has substantial equity investments in dozens of publicly traded companies. It holds more than $70 billion worth of cash and fixed-income securities, including Treasury bonds, municipal bonds, corporate bonds, and mortgage-backed securities. This certainly appears to constitute a well-diversified portfolio. In reality, however, even a portfolio as varied as this is more concentrated than finance theory recommends. And just a few years earlier, Berkshire's investments were far more concentrated than this.

More Return, Less Risk

Whatever Buffett may think of diversification, the reason finance professionals aggressively promote the idea is because diversification reduces risk. Indeed, the more diversified a portfolio, the greater the reduction in risk. By diversifying your portfolio, you minimize the impact that any one stock will have if it unexpectedly blows up.

Of course, there are other ways to reduce risk. For example, you could easily eliminate investment risk altogether by not investing at all. But reducing risk is not the sole purpose of diversification. The real goal is to generate as much return as you can for as little risk as possible.

This is not some arbitrary harebrained idea cooked up in an ivory tower. There is sound mathematical reasoning behind the concept, as well as a lot of common sense. The mathematical reasoning has to do with a statistical measure known as *covariance,* which reveals how two variables, such as the returns on two stocks, change in relation to one another. The *correlation coefficient* standardizes the covariance so that it is always bound between −1 and +1. This makes it easier to interpret.

At this point, you might be shaking your head and thinking, "Do I have to take a course in higher mathematics just to read a book about Warren Buffett?" You will be relieved to learn that the answer is no. But going through this process will help you appreciate Buffett's simpler, commonsense approach to investing.

If the correlation coefficient between two stocks is equal to +1, then the two stocks are said to be perfectly positively correlated. For example, if one rises 10 percent in value, the other might rise 5 percent in value. If the first falls 10 percent in value, the other falls 5 percent in value. There is no point in holding both stocks in a portfolio because they always move in the same direction and in exact proportion with one another.

At the opposite extreme, if the correlation coefficient is equal to −1, then the two stocks are perfectly negatively correlated. If one goes up 10 percent, the other might fall 8 percent. If the first falls 10 percent, the second rises 8 percent. If held in a portfolio, they provide a perfect hedge because they always move in opposite directions and in perfect proportion with one another.

Alternatively, if the correlation coefficient is equal to zero, the two stocks are perfectly uncorrelated. This means that knowing what one stock does provides no hint of what the other might do.

Of course, correlation coefficients can take on any value between -1 and $+1$. Resorting to some rather complicated mathematics, any finance professor can prove that as long as the correlation coefficient between two stocks is less than $+1$, there are benefits to owning both stocks. Furthermore, the smaller the correlation coefficient, the greater are the benefits. The explanation of why this happens is fairly technical. However, it basically boils down to the fact that the expected return of a portfolio is a weighted average of the expected returns of each of the stocks in the portfolio, but the risk of a portfolio is not a weighted average of the risks of each of the stocks. Mathematically speaking, this is what diversification is all about.

As you might suspect, Buffett does not spend much time calculating correlation coefficients. He does not have to; and neither do you if you just exercise some common sense. Because in the real world correlation coefficients are always less than $+1$, common sense is all you really need. You must also recognize that, just as the theory dictates, there are always benefits to diversifying your portfolio. What exactly are these benefits? It can all be summed up by the following statement:

A properly diversified portfolio provides the highest level of expected return for any given amount of risk,

or the lowest amount of risk for any given level of expected return.

No doubt some investors believe that finance professors who
dream up this kind of stuff live in some theoretical universe that
bears little resemblance to reality. After all, when professors talk,
people tend to fall asleep. When Warren Buffett talks, they listen
very attentively. This is because professors rely on mathematics
with all kinds of complicated formulas to make their points. Buffett famously makes his points using ordinary common sense. Professors prefer complexity. Buffett prefers simplicity.

And although the aforementioned statement might seem rather
simple, there are actually several complicated concepts behind it.
First, there is the word "properly." It implies that not all diversified portfolios are *properly* diversified. Indeed, according to the
theory, a properly diversified portfolio is one that includes all
stocks. Yes, that's right. All stocks! (To be more precise, it actually
includes all *assets,* but since this is a book about Warren Buffett,
in the interest of simplicity, we will limit the discussion to
stocks.)

Furthermore, the only difference between one properly diversified portfolio and another properly diversified portfolio is the proportion of funds invested in each stock. Two portfolios might
include the same stocks, but they are not identical unless the same
proportional amount of money is invested in each.

The statement also mentions "expected" returns. It does not
talk about actual returns. This is because no one knows for sure
ahead of time what the actual return of a stock or a portfolio of
stocks will be. Therefore, the projected return must be estimated.
In part, this estimate is based on how much risk is involved. Which
brings us to another fundamental rule of modern portfolio theory:

the greater the risk, the greater the expected return. If one properly diversified portfolio is riskier than another properly diversified portfolio, it is also expected to provide a greater return.

Indeed, "risk" is another important variable in the diversification discussion (and in the statement above). Earlier in this chapter we learned that Buffett defines risk as the possibility of losing money. But there are other ways to define risk. Financial researchers focus on volatility. Indeed, it turns out that finance theory is talking about a very specific kind of risk called total risk, which is measured by another mathematical variable called the *variance,* or its square root, the *standard deviation.* (Once again, do not get intimidated by these mathematical concepts. You do not need a math degree to understand this book. By going through this process, however, you will be all the more grateful for Buffett's commonsense approach to investing.)

Interestingly, finance theory considers a stock to be risky if it shows a tendency to go up or down by a large amount. Buffett thinks this is silly. After all, why should a stock that goes up be considered risky? Buffett only worries about the risk that a stock will fall. The theory is focused on total risk, but Buffett worries only about downside risk.

Buffett Relies on Common Sense

Finance theory holds that diversification is good because it reduces total risk. Furthermore, the theory says that the smaller the correlation coefficient, the greater the reduction in risk. Buffett knows there are lots of problems with this theory. One big one is that correlation coefficients are not static. They are changing all the time. Sometimes they change quite rapidly.

Many investors believe that diversification can bulletproof their portfolios. Some stocks may go down, but others will go up.

As a result, the overall portfolio is protected. Some investors even think a properly diversified portfolio will protect them from a market sell-off. Unfortunately, things do not always work this way. Investors panic during sell-offs. They start selling indiscriminately. Stocks that were previously thought to be uncorrelated with one another all fall at once. Even portfolios that include foreign securities suffer during a panic sell-off. Ironically, diversification often provides the least amount of protection when that protection is needed the most.

Fortunately, panic sell-offs are rare events. Barring such unusual events, it turns out that diversification can indeed reduce the risk of a portfolio. Diversification actually works pretty well under most market conditions when correlation coefficients, while not perfectly constant, are at least fairly stable. This is precisely why some sophisticated investors hunt for correlated stocks. Alternatively, many hedge funds specialize in looking for uncorrelated assets, and then taking long and short positions in them. (A short position involves borrowing and selling stock you do not own with the intention of buying it back later at a lower price. In a short position, the value of the investment goes up when the price of the stock goes down. This is exactly the opposite of what most investors want.)

The vast majority of investors, however, do not sit around calculating correlation coefficients before deciding which stocks to add to their portfolios. Neither does Buffett. Quantitative analysts may do it on a regular basis, but few, if any, ordinary investors actually compute correlation coefficients before making investment decisions. The good news is they don't have to.

Here is a simple example that shows why in most cases common sense—one of Warren Buffett's favorite concepts—works just as well. Suppose you like General Motors and decide to buy some of its stock. If GM is the only stock you own, you obviously have a very risky portfolio. Indeed, GM is susceptible to all kinds of risks. Some of these risks might affect all stocks. Some risks, however, are specific only to GM. If the economy were to go into recession, chances are the entire stock market would suffer. But if GM fails to sign a favorable contract with its union, this is a risk specific to GM. The company's union troubles are not likely to affect the value of many other stocks.

Fortunately, you can reduce your exposure to some of the risks specific to GM by adding another stock to your portfolio. Obviously it does not make much sense to buy shares of Ford Motor Company. After all, Ford and GM are in the same industry and are exposed to many of the same risks. In fact, Ford must negotiate with the very same unions as GM. If you really want to reduce the risk of your portfolio, you would be better off adding the stock of a company from some unrelated industry. A good candidate might be a blue-chip technology stock like Microsoft.

No doubt the professionals would agree, but not because they relied on common sense. They would say that GM and Microsoft make a better portfolio than GM and Ford because the correlation coefficient between GM and Microsoft is smaller than the correlation coefficient between GM and Ford. In fact, for a consulting fee, any finance professor would be happy to prove it to you by doing some regression analysis and actually computing the numbers. But this level of complexity is not really necessary. You could instead just do what Warren Buffett does all the time—exercise some common sense.

Buffett does not own Microsoft or GM, but he knows intuitively that adding Microsoft to a portfolio consisting of GM will reduce risk to a greater extent than adding Ford to that same portfolio. After all, Microsoft and GM are in completely different industries. They are not going to have a lot of risk factors in common. If the price of tires goes up, that will certainly affect GM's profits. But higher tire prices are not likely to affect Microsoft's profits. On the other hand, GM and Ford have much in common. There is a good chance that what affects one will also affect the other.

Is More Better or Is More Just More?

Suppose you decide to buy some Microsoft stock for your portfolio. Can you reduce risk further by buying a third stock? Of course you can. Ideally, you should find a stock that is not correlated with either GM or Microsoft. Perhaps a utility company such as Duke Energy would fit the bill.

Risk reduction depends not just on how correlated the stocks in a portfolio are with one another; it also depends on how many stocks are in the portfolio. It turns out the more stocks you add, the greater the reduction in risk.

So far, Buffett and those who prefer a more mathematical approach have much in common. However, differences arise when you ask how many stocks are enough. True believers in modern portfolio theory—let us call them the extremists—say there is no limit. Just keep adding stocks. The more, the merrier. Remember, according to the extremists, every stock belongs in a properly diversified portfolio. Indeed, they would probably advise investors to forget about buying individual stocks altogether. Instead, they would tell investors to put their money into index funds. An index fund is a mutual fund or exchange traded fund (ETF)[3] that invests in a large basket of stocks that are included in a particular market index. For example, an index fund that tracks the Standard & Poor's 500 Index includes all five hundred stocks.

Warren Buffett is not likely to take this kind of advice. He certainly is not going to use Berkshire's money to buy as many stocks as he possibly can. He would consider this idea ridiculous for two simple reasons. First, even if the theory is correct and all known stocks belong in a diversified portfolio, this is not practicable in the real world. Second, even if one could somehow manage to buy some shares of every conceivable company, it would be more prudent to buy only the good stocks and avoid the bad ones, assuming of course that you are capable of discerning the difference.

Let us take a closer look at each argument. Of course, it would be tremendously difficult, if not impossible, to individually purchase shares of every public company that exists. But these days, you can come pretty close to doing that by purchasing index funds. There are numerous mutual funds and exchange traded funds available that track just about every imaginable index. It seems a new one comes to market every day. If you were to buy a sufficient number and variety of these index funds, you could actually get exposure to the vast majority of stocks without directly buying any of the stocks themselves. These days it is quite possible to get exposure to almost all U.S. equities in this manner. The extremists would applaud this strategy.

You will probably be surprised to learn that so would Buffett—at least for ordinary investors. It turns out that the world's greatest stock picker thinks ordinary investors should forget about picking stocks altogether. Instead, the man who made a fortune by holding only a few choice stocks thinks ordinary investors should buy index funds. He said during a talk at the University of Florida in October 1998, "Maybe more than 99 percent of people who invest should extensively diversify." He even wrote in his

2003 letter to shareholders, "Index funds that are very low cost (such as Vanguard's) are investor-friendly by definition and are the best selection for most of those who wish to own equities."

These remarks must come as a shock to all the Buffett aficionados who have been schooled to believe that the best investment strategy is to buy shares in only a few good companies. Buffett and his top lieutenant, Charlie Munger, are even on record as ridiculing diversification and extolling the virtues of portfolio concentration. Almost every book written about Buffett stresses his disdain for diversification and his preference for concentration. So what gives? What explains this apparent contradiction? What is Buffett's real message?

Buffett is saying that diversification is not for him, but it is perfectly fine for almost everyone else. As you might expect, Berkshire Hathaway owns absolutely no index funds. No doubt Buffett would consider it ridiculous to use Berkshire's money to buy index funds. Yet he obviously believes that ordinary investors should do as he says and not as he does.

During that same talk at the University of Florida he went on to explain that diversification is a terrible idea for those who really understand how to evaluate businesses. He told the audience that if you are really good at evaluating businesses, then owning about six companies is all the diversification you need.

As you might imagine, Buffett's personal holdings are not very diversified at all. In fact, the vast majority of his wealth is invested in Berkshire Hathaway stock. And for years, Berkshire's holdings could not be considered well diversified. Yet Berkshire has been going through a transformation. Today, Berkshire's portfolio of investments is more diversified than at any time in the company's history. When you think about it, you will realize that it has to be.

Berkshire has grown so large and has so much money to invest, it can't help but diversify. Berkshire's phenomenal growth has forced Buffett to make a major strategy change. Berkshire's current investment holdings certainly seem to be signaling a shift in strategy from concentration to diversification. While this new approach makes Berkshire a less risky company, at the same time, it could also depress future returns. In fact, Buffett himself has warned that Berkshire will not be able to generate the same kinds of returns in the future as it has in the past. It is simply too large to do so.

It Happens on the Margin

If Buffett is not as opposed to diversification as his reputation would have us believe, why did he wait so long to diversify Berkshire's holdings? One answer, as we have already seen, is that he did not have to. When Berkshire was a smaller company, it was easier to concentrate its investments. Now that it is so large, concentration becomes more difficult.

But there is more to the story than that. Recall why the experts say diversification is a good thing: because diversification reduces risk. Furthermore, the more stocks you put into a portfolio, the greater the reduction in risk. That reality raises an important question: how many stocks does an investor really need to own?

Buffett realized long ago that the greatest degree of risk reduction occurs when the number of stocks in a portfolio is small. If you own just one stock, you can reduce risk a great deal simply by adding another stock to your portfolio. But if you already own several dozen stocks, buying one more hardly reduces risk at all. After a while, you might even find that the marginal reduction in risk that comes from adding one more stock to your portfolio is not worth the added trouble and expense of having to track an additional company. Even mutual fund managers find that expenses go up as they add more stocks to their funds. This is another one of those complicated theoretical concepts that Buffett understands intuitively.

Because the marginal reduction in risk declines as you add more stocks to a portfolio, you might reasonably wonder when enough is enough. While there is no magic number, it becomes clear that after a while it makes little sense to keep adding more stocks. Yet there is much disagreement in the research community about how many stocks are enough. The modern portfolio theory extremists say an investor's portfolio should include all stocks. They want to see as many as possible. Moderates have no problem living with a finite number. Some say one hundred stocks, some say fifty. Some even believe only twenty stocks are sufficient.

What does Warren Buffett think? Earlier in this chapter, we learned that Buffett believes that owning just six stocks is enough for those who know what they are doing. Fortunately, we can examine Berkshire Hathaway's holdings to see if Buffett practices what he preaches. After all, Berkshire is really a holding company. It is much like a mutual fund or investment company. Berkshire is a company that owns other companies. Some companies it fully owns. In others, it has large equity stakes. Berkshire is an active acquirer, so the number of companies it owns is constantly rising. According to its Web site and filings with the Securities and Exchange Commission, at last count Berkshire owned about seventy subsidiary companies and had significant stakes in about forty publicly traded companies. Tables 1.1 and 1.2 (page 30) list just a sampling of some of Berkshire's better-known holdings.[4]

Table 1.1

Some of Berkshire's Better-Known Subsidiaries

GEICO
General Re
National Indemnity
Benjamin Moore & Co.
Borsheim's Fine Jewelry
Clayton Homes
Fruit of the Loom
Johns-Manville
Jordan's Furniture
Nebraska Furniture Mart
NetJets
See's Candies
Shaw Industries
Wesco Financial Corp.
Intl. Dairy Queen

Because the subsidiaries are wholly owned, it is difficult to place an accurate value on them. However, it is easy to determine the market values of all of the publicly traded companies. For example, Berkshire owns 200 million shares of Coca-Cola, which at the end of 2006 were worth $9.7 billion. At the other extreme, Berkshire's position in Pier 1 Imports (not listed in the table) was worth only $8.8 million.

Given all of Berkshire's wholly owned subsidiaries and publicly traded companies, is it fair to say that Buffett now believes it makes sense to own a rather large number of stocks? After all,

Table 1.2

Market Values of Berkshire's Top Ten Public Stock Holdings (as of December 2006)

COMPANY	MARKET VALUE ($ millions)
Coca-Cola	9,650
American Express	9,198
Wells Fargo	7,758
Procter & Gamble	6,427
Moody's Corp.	3,315
PetroChina	3,313
Tesco	1,820
Anheuser-Busch	1,792
Johnson & Johnson	1,409
ConocoPhillips	1,291

Berkshire's portfolio appears to be quite diversified. It certainly is more diversified than it was just a few years earlier. Perhaps Buffett has finally concluded that broad diversification is good not just for the masses—it is good for Berkshire, too.

However, that would be an erroneous conclusion. According to the modern portfolio theory extremists, Berkshire's portfolio is still much too concentrated. The extremists not only would say that Berkshire has an insufficient number of holdings, they also would point out that its holdings are exceedingly lopsided in value. Indeed, the bulk of Berkshire's portfolio is invested in a rather small number of companies, and a relatively small amount of money is invested in all the others. For example, as of December 2006, Berkshire's stock holdings had a total market value of $61.5 billion. Yet more than half that amount, $33 billion, was invested in just four companies: Coca-Cola, American Express, Wells Fargo, and Procter & Gamble. The remaining $28 billion was invested in at least thirty-six other companies.

Nonetheless, it cannot be denied that Berkshire's holdings are much more diversified today than at any time in its history. Back in the early days when Berkshire was just a shadow of itself, it was invested almost solely in textiles and insurance. Even as recently as 1998, when the company had already become a huge phenomenon with a market cap of about $100 billion, its holdings were not nearly as diversified as they are today. In 1998, Berkshire had a healthy number of subsidiary companies, but it disclosed equity positions in just eight publicly traded companies: American Express, Coca-Cola, Gillette, M&T Bank Corp., PS Group Holdings, SunTrust Banks, The Washington Post Company, and Wesco Financial Corp.

Even the moderates in academia and the professional investment communities would have agreed that eight was simply too few a number for proper diversification. They would also have pointed out that several of those eight companies even operated in the same industry, resulting in little diversification. They would have argued that Buffett was exposing his shareholders to way too much risk. Keep in mind, however, that the academics focus on total risk. Buffett focuses on downside risk. The academics will respond by saying that diversification provides protection against downside risk and will keep you from going broke. All too often, however, they forget to mention that diversification can also prevent you from becoming filthy rich.

If you look at *Forbes* magazine's list of the 400 Richest

Americans, you will not find many who got there by holding extensively diversified portfolios. The top ten members from 2007 are listed in Table 1.3. Bill Gates and Larry Ellison made their fortunes in software by creating Microsoft and Oracle, respectively. Sheldon Adelson and Kirk Kerkorian owe much of their wealth to the gaming and entertainment industries. Larry Page and Sergey Brin are the cofounders of Google. Michael Dell's money was generated from his eponymous computer company. The Koch brothers inherited their wealth from their father, who founded Koch Industries.

Table 1.3
Forbes 2007 Richest Americans[5]

NAME	ESTIMATED WEALTH	PRIMARY COMPANY
Bill Gates	$59.0 billion	Microsoft
Warren Buffett	$52.0 billion	Berkshire Hathaway
Sheldon Adelson	$28.0 billion	Las Vegas Sands
Larry Ellison	$26.0 billion	Oracle
Sergey Brin	$18.5 billion	Google
Larry Page	$18.5 billion	Google
Kirk Kerkorian	$18.0 billion	MGM Mirage
Michael Dell	$17.2 billion	Dell
Charles Koch	$17.0 billion	Koch Industries
David Koch	$17.0 billion	Koch Industries

As with many of the megarich, Buffett's wealth is primarily tied to just one company: Berkshire Hathaway. But Berkshire is not like most companies. Berkshire is really an investment company. When you buy a share of Berkshire common stock, you are actually buying an interest in all the companies Berkshire owns. While it may be true that Buffett's investment in Berkshire is much more concentrated than what modern portfolio theory recommends, it is considerably more diversified than the holdings of the vast majority of America's billionaires.

Even so, diversification is not what made Buffett rich. His wealth is the result of concentration in a relatively few companies. At the end of 2006, Berkshire's market capitalization stood at about $170 billion. For an investment company that large, even a 100-stock portfolio might be considered too concentrated—especially if the bulk of the money is invested in just a handful of companies and stocks. As we saw earlier, Berkshire has huge investments in a rather small number of companies, and relatively small investments in all the others. It is particularly exposed to the insurance industry. Indeed, Berkshire's insurance businesses produced about one fourth of its revenues and one half of its profits in 2006. There are many mutual funds just a fraction of Berkshire's size with holdings of a hundred stocks or more. But few, if any, can boast the kind of returns Berkshire has produced over the long term.

Furthermore, it could be argued that Buffett's strategy of selective concentration actually allows him to control risk. When Buffett buys a stock (through Berkshire), he does not buy just a few hundred shares as the rest of us might. He usually makes a large enough investment to immediately show up on the company's radar screen. His investments are large enough to allow him to influence managerial decisions. For example, Berkshire owns more than 15 percent of all the outstanding shares of Coca-Cola. In fact, Buffett sat on Coca-Cola's board for seventeen years. Although he is no longer a director, you can bet management is not going to ignore his advice should he choose to render it. You can also bet that Coca-Cola's CEO will return Buffett's phone calls as soon as possible.

Yet just because a strategy of concentration has worked well for Warren Buffett, it is not safe to assume it will work well for you. Even if you have a few million dollars to invest and you choose to put it all in just one publicly traded company, chances are it will not be enough to get you noticed. Buffett would advise you to diversify your investment holdings. However, if you are determined to follow a strategy of concentration, you might want to consider an entirely different route altogether, such as using your money to start your own business. This is because concentration can help control risk only when it allows you to shape the company's business plan and gives you some influence over managerial decisions. Buffett believes that if you can't invest enough money to have some say in how the company's capital is to be deployed, you are better off diversifying your portfolio.

Buy Only Good Stocks

Let us now turn to the second argument we mentioned earlier against excessive diversification. If a properly diversified portfolio includes all stocks, it necessarily must include both good and bad ones. Would it not be better to buy and hold only the good stocks? Obviously, the answer is yes. The problem, of course, is being able to identify the good stocks. While any novice will tell you that good stocks are the ones that go up, the trick is finding the good stocks *before* they go up. This is where superior analysis skills are required, and this is where Buffett excels.

It is impossible to write a book about Warren Buffett without mentioning Benjamin Graham. Graham is the author of *The Intelligent Investor* (1949) and the lead author of *Security Analysis* (1934). He was Buffett's teacher at Columbia University's Graduate School of Business. He later employed Buffett in his investment firm. Graham taught Buffett the virtues and drawbacks of diversification. Graham taught Buffett security analysis and stock selection. Graham taught Buffett to favor large, conservatively financed, and undervalued companies with a consistent record of paying dividends.

Philip Fisher was another investing genius who influenced Buffett's thinking. Fisher taught at Stanford's Graduate School of Business and authored *Common Stocks and Uncommon Profits* (1958). He made a fortune buying shares of Motorola in 1955 and holding them until his death in 2004. Fisher taught Buffett to learn everything he could about a business, including its vendors, competitors, and customers. Fisher also taught Buffett to keep his holdings concentrated and to buy only what he understands.

Thanks to mentors like Graham and Fisher, Buffett developed into an outstanding stock picker. Yet modern portfolio theory extremists say picking stocks is a waste of time. As evidence, they point to a plethora of research that concludes that most professional money managers cannot consistently beat benchmarks such as the Standard & Poor's 500 over long periods of time.

They also point to studies that conclude that asset allocation is more important than security selection. As we learned earlier, *asset allocation* refers to the process of deciding how exposed an investor should be to each of the various asset classes. Asset allocation goes hand in hand with diversification. Asset allocation is simply diversification across asset classes rather than diversification within asset classes.

A simple asset allocation model might consider only three asset classes: stocks, bonds, and cash. More complicated models would include other asset classes as well, such as real estate, commodities, currencies, precious metals, and alternatives. There are also sub-classes to choose from. For example, how much of the money devoted to equities should be in domestic equities? How much should be in foreign stocks? Which foreign markets should be included? How much should be in large-caps, midcaps, and small-caps? What about bonds? How much should be in government bonds, corporate bonds, municipal bonds, and non-dollar denominated bonds?

As you can see, asset allocation involves making decisions about what proportion of a portfolio belongs in each asset class. Furthermore, what is right for one investor may not be right for another. A professional investment adviser would have to consider each individual investor's objectives and constraints. These might include factors such as taxes and the ability or inability to tolerate risk.

In addition, decisions have to be made about rebalancing. For example, suppose you decide 60 percent of your portfolio should be allocated to equities and 40 percent to bonds. If stocks rally while bonds fall, you might soon find yourself with 70 percent stocks and only 30 percent bonds. Should you rebalance your portfolio to take it back to the initial 60-40 target mix? If so, how often should you rebalance? Keep in mind that if you rebalance frequently, your trading costs will be high. But if you rebalance infrequently, your portfolio allocation might tilt way off target.

These are the kinds of questions investment advisers think about. Many experts agree that when it comes to constructing portfolios, asset allocation is much more important than security selection. One of the first and most widely cited studies was conducted by Gary Brinson, Randolph Hood, and Gilbert Beebower.[6] These researchers studied pension funds and concluded that more than 90 percent of the variation in quarterly returns over time was explained by asset allocation. Less than 10 percent was explained by market timing or security selection.

Based on results from studies such as this, one would conclude that if investors really wanted to do themselves a service, they would be better off thinking more seriously about how much of their money to invest in each asset class and worrying less about which specific securities to buy. Most investors spend too little time on asset allocation. They would benefit by thinking more seriously about how much money to allocate to stocks, bonds, real estate, cash, and other asset classes.

Vanguard's founder Jack Bogle agrees that asset allocation is more important than security selection. But he also points out that asset allocation is not a particularly difficult or time-consuming exercise. Indeed, asset allocation decisions are relatively simple for very long-term investors such as Warren Buffett who are not concerned about quarter-to-quarter volatility.

What exactly is long-term? Some investors think of the long term as two or three years. For others, long-term means five or ten years. But when Buffett talks about the long term, he is usually thinking decades, not years. If he makes an investment today, he does not worry too much about what it might be worth next year. In some cases, he may not even care. Instead, Buffett focuses on what the investment could be worth ten, twenty, or even thirty years in the future. He advises investors to buy stocks as if the market will remain closed for the next ten years. That speaks volumes about his attitude and time frame. Buffett has even said "forever" is an appropriate amount of time to hold a stock.

Although Buffett does not engage in rebalancing too often, that does not mean he is always wedded to his positions. He is certainly smart enough to know that it rarely pays to be obstinate. He has been known to change his mind and sell sooner than his reputation might lead you to expect. Indeed, there are many investments Buffett has "flipped" in five years or less.[7] But the fact remains: Buffett rarely enters an investment with a short-term exit strategy in mind. He stressed as much in his 2005 letter to shareholders when he wrote, "Unlike many business buyers, Berkshire has no 'exit strategy.' We buy to keep."[8]

According to Jeremy Siegel's classic book, *Stocks for the Long Run*,[9] Buffett's long-term focus makes a good deal of sense. Siegel found that from 1871 to 1992, there were absolutely no thirty-year periods of time (no matter what starting point you choose) during which stocks failed to outperform bonds. Even for investment horizons of only ten years, stocks outperformed bonds more than 80 percent of the time. So if, like Buffett, you invest for the very long run, you do not need to spend an excessive amount of time thinking about asset allocation. Like Buffett, you certainly should hold some cash and own some bonds, but if you are truly a long-term investor, you should have a healthy dose of stocks in your portfolio. Indeed, Buffett would probably agree that 80 percent or more is an appropriate allocation of stocks for the long-term investor.

Of course, if you know you will be in need of large sums of money three to five years from now to pay for college tuition or to purchase a new home, you must take that into consideration. You should also keep enough cash available to meet unforeseen expenses and emergencies, or to take advantage of promising opportunities that might unexpectedly arise. Assuming you have planned for such contingencies—and are not betting the proverbial farm—then allocating the bulk of your long-term investments to stocks makes a lot of sense.

Like Buffett, you would want to buy only good stocks. Keep in mind, however, that no one—not even Buffett—has a perfect track record. Buffett, like most investors, has made some truly awful investments. The 8 million shares of Pier 1 Imports, purchased in 2004, provides a recent example. The stock fell 70 percent soon after Buffett's initial purchase. But Buffett did not take advantage of the stock's plunge by buying more shares and averaging down his cost as he so often does when a stock he likes falls in price. Instead, he chose to take his losses and began paring back on his Pier 1 holdings. Although Buffett prefers to invest for the long term, it appears that he quickly lost faith in this particular stock.

The point is that your goal should not be to make lots of money—or even a little money—on every single investment. Like Buffett, you should strive to earn market-beating returns on your overall portfolio over the long run. You want to be right more often than you are wrong. You want to make enough money on your good calls to more than offset what you will inevitably lose on your bad ones. In order to do that, you need to know what works best—but not just in the long run. You should also know what works best in the short run. We will learn about investing in the long and short run in the pages ahead.

KEY TAKEAWAYS: CHAPTER 1

- Diversification is perhaps the single most important concept in investment management. All competent and responsible financial advisers will urge their clients to diversify. However, diversification does not have to be an all-or-nothing strategy. Buffett's personal wealth is the result of concentration—not diversification. *If you have a certain level of investment expertise and are capable of analyzing companies, or if you have access to advisers who possess these skills, you should avoid diversifying excessively. But if you lack the time and expertise to thoroughly research companies and learn everything about them, you should diversify extensively. Buffett suggests using index funds for those who want to diversify.*

- Early in its history, Berkshire Hathaway was an extremely concentrated investment company. Even in the late 1990s, it had relatively few subsidiary companies and owned only about half a dozen stocks. Eventually, however, Berkshire came to own dozens of stocks and about seventy subsidiary companies. Although Berkshire is more diversified than it has ever been, it remains less diversified than what finance theory recommends. *Even if you start building wealth with a concentrated approach, you should pay more attention to diversification as your wealth grows.*

- The key to diversification is finding uncorrelated assets. Yet a simple commonsense approach often works just as well as a more complicated quantitative approach that requires the computation of correlation coefficients. *When adding stocks to your portfolio, avoid those that are exposed to the same risks. A properly constructed portfolio that contains just a few stocks can often provide as much risk reduction as a poorly constructed portfolio that has a much larger number of stocks. Buffett says a six-stock portfolio provides sufficient diversification for those who know what they are doing.*

- Most active investors spend a tremendous amount of time trying to pick winning stocks. The evidence, however, suggests they should worry more about asset allocation than security selection. However, long-term investors like Buffett find that settling upon a proper asset allocation is not a particularly difficult exercise. *Spend at least as much time thinking about how much of your money to put into stocks and other asset classes as you do thinking about which specific stocks to buy. But if you are truly a long-term investor, make sure you have a healthy dose of equities in your portfolio.*

2

The Undervalued Buffett

Two people looking at the same set of facts, moreover—and that includes Charlie [Munger] and me—will almost inevitably come up with at least slightly different intrinsic value figures.

—Warren Buffett, 2005

When the reporters at cable business network CNBC interview a money manager, they almost always label him or her as a value manager or a growth manager. They give the impression that value and growth are diametrically opposed investment philosophies. Whether they manage separate accounts or mutual funds, money managers are almost always categorized in one camp or the other. Indeed, whole mutual funds are classified in a similar fashion. A mutual fund's prospectus will tell you if it is a large-cap domestic value fund, small-cap international growth fund, mid-cap global blend fund, or any number of possible combinations.

Buffett Likes Value, but He Also Buys Growth

Warren Buffett is widely believed to be a value investor. Whether he really is or is not, however, depends on how you actually define value. Buffett does have a history of buying companies that look incredibly cheap in hindsight. Sometimes he goes after companies that have sustained a considerable price drop. His investment strategies certainly seem to be consistent with a value bent. However, it is also true that many of the stocks Buffett has purchased over the years have exhibited tremendous growth.

Confusion results because it is not always clear exactly how the terms value and growth are defined. The traditional methodology is to focus on price multiples. The most common price multiples are price-to-earnings (P/E), price-to-cash-flow (P/CF), price-to-book (P/B), and price-to-sales (P/S). Stocks that have low price multiples are said to be *value stocks.* Those with high multiples are said to be *growth stocks.*

Let's Google The Washington Post

To understand Buffett's thinking, let us take a close look at two rather popular stocks. Google became one of the hottest stocks on the market immediately after it went public in August 2004 at an offering price of $85 per share. The stock surged 18 percent and closed above $100 on the very first day of trading. It never looked back. Three years after going public, shares of Google had appreciated more than eight times in price. You would be hard-pressed to find other stocks that have done as well in such a short amount of time. Yet Warren Buffett has never owned Google.

In the mid-1970s, however, Buffett purchased shares of The Washington Post Company on Berkshire Hathaway's behalf. Like Google, the Post has also been an outstanding performer. In fact, it is one of the best investments Buffett has ever made—at least on a percentage-return basis. Berkshire's initial investment of about $11 million in the Post was worth $1.3 billion at the end of 2006.

That comes out to an 11,609 percent return—and that's not counting dividends.

As shown in Figures 2.1 and 2.2 (page 46), if you place the price graphs of Google and the Post right next to each other you will see that they look quite similar. There is, of course, one major difference between the two. Take a look at the scale on the horizontal axes. Google's extraordinary gains were generated over a much shorter period of time. It took the Post a decade to produce the kind of stock chart pattern Google generated in just three years. The Post's chart also reveals that the stock has not done very well in recent periods. In fact, if you look closely, you will see that the Post's stock price began to weaken just around the same time Google went public. This is not just coincidence.

Figure 2.1

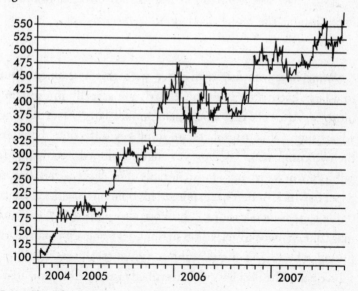

Price Chart for Google *(Source: Telemet America)*

Figure 2.2

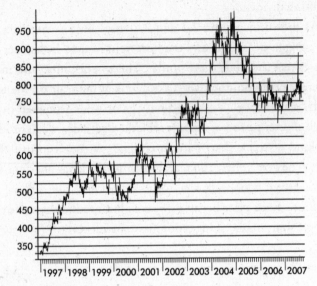

Price Chart for The Washington Post *(Source: Telemet America)*

Some investors might disagree with this assessment, but to a large extent the Post and Google are actually in the same business. After all, they both make money largely from selling advertising. Of course, there are some key differences between the two companies. The Post is a traditional media company. It publishes newspapers—most notably *The Washington Post,* a paper in which Buffett has expressed his opinions on critical issues on at least four occasions. The Post also publishes *Newsweek* magazine. It owns six television stations. Its Cable One subsidiary provides basic and digital cable services to almost a million subscribers. The Post has even diversified into the education arena by purchasing Kaplan, the test preparation company that helps students prepare for college admission tests as well as professional licensing exams.

Google, on the other hand, is an Internet company. It is a newfangled business based on a technology its founders created that allows users to search the Internet for all kinds of information. Google's technology presents the results of an online search in fractions of a second. Google is not the only search engine on the Web. There are a number of well-known competitors, including Microsoft and Yahoo!. There are also several lesser-known competitors. But Google quickly became the premier search engine with the largest market share by far. Google also branched out into online videos. It began by creating its own video technology that allowed users to post and share videos. Then it purchased YouTube for $1.65 billion. Even though YouTube had no revenues, it was by far the dominant player in the online video space. Compared to traditional media companies such as The Washington Post, Google is said to be in a new and exciting business. Internet analysts and technology experts alike claim Google has revolutionized the way people access information.

Clearly, Google and The Washington Post have some similarities as well as a number of differences. As mentioned previously, one critical difference is that the Post has been a core holding in Berkshire's portfolio for many years, but Google is a stock Berkshire has never owned. Furthermore, there is a very good chance that under Buffett's control Berkshire will never own Google. Why not? Take a look at Table 2.1 (page 48). It displays some of the price multiples for these two companies.

Table 2.1

**Price Multiples for The Washington Post and Google
(September 2007)**

PRICE MULTIPLE	WASHINGTON POST	GOOGLE
Price-earnings	25.4	48.2
Price–cash flow	13.2	40.4
Price-book	2.3	9.0
Price-sales	1.9	13.1

Google was selling for $570 per share when these figures were compiled. The Washington Post was selling for $800 per share. Based on price, the Post seems to be the more expensive stock, but Buffett would be quick to remind us that price alone does not make one stock more expensive than another. Although the Post has the higher market price, it is actually a much cheaper stock because, as shown in Table 2.1, its price multiples are much smaller than Google's.

Multiples are extremely important measures in financial analysis because they put price in perspective. Multiples tell us how much investors are really willing to pay for a stock. As Table 2.1 makes abundantly clear, investors were willing to pay much more for Google than for the Post. In fact, they were willing to pay 48.2 times earnings for Google, but only 25.4 times earnings for the Post. They were willing to pay 13.1 times sales for Google, but only 1.9 times sales for the Post. As an astute buyer, Buffett wants to pay as little as possible for any investment. Stocks with low price multiples are more likely to pique his interest.

Why were investors keen to pay so much more for a share of Google than for a share of the Post? Buffett will tell you the answer has to do with growth. To be more precise, it has to do with *expected* growth. At the time these figures were compiled, both companies were expected to grow revenues and earnings. But Google was expected to grow them at a much faster rate. In fact, analysts were projecting Google's earnings to grow more than 30 percent annually over the next five years. The corresponding five-year expected earnings growth rate for The Washington Post was just 8 percent.

Investors were willing to pay more for Google because they were willing to pay more for growth. There is nothing wrong with this. Buffett himself has sometimes shown a willingness to pay a premium for growth. He may prefer to buy stocks with low multiples, but he will certainly consider buying a higher-multiple stock if he is convinced the growth rate justifies the premium. This is a perfectly reasonable and logical thing to do. After all, a company with a high expected growth rate is worth more than an otherwise identical company that is expected to have little or no growth. Of course, investors may debate how much more the high-growth company is worth, but there is no question it is worth more than a low-growth company.

If this is not immediately obvious to you, consider this example. Two stocks, A and B, both have $2 per share in earnings. Stock A is in a rather boring, slow-growth business. Its earnings are expected to grow 5 percent per year. So in five years A's earnings should be $2.55 per share. But stock B's earnings are expected to grow 20 percent per year. In five years, stock B's earnings should be almost $5 per share. If these stocks are equally risky and you could buy either one today for the same price, which would you purchase?

Obviously, you should purchase B. Stock B is worth more than stock A because it has a higher expected growth rate. Now let us complicate things a bit. Would you still be willing to buy stock B if it were selling for a higher price than stock A? Your answer should now depend on how much higher that price is. If it is just a little higher, then yes, you should still prefer B. But if it is a lot higher, then A may be the better investment.

The problem, as Buffett sees it, is that expectations for high-growth companies often get way out of hand. Their stock prices can sometimes get much too high to justify buying them. Buffett knows investors have a tendency to extrapolate recent events into the future. When things are going well, they like to believe the good times will continue for quite some time. As a result, they often end up paying too much for the stock.

Likewise, when things are going poorly, investors sometimes give up hope. They can't imagine that things might get better. Buffett loves this situation. He realizes that when this happens, a stock's price can sink much lower than it should, making it a real bargain. Some of Berkshire's most successful investments were made when other investors had given up hope. Buffett has even said that long-term investors should not be rooting for stock prices to rise. They should instead be wishing they fall so they can buy more shares at a lower price. Buffett has said the only time you should want stock prices to go up is when you are ready to sell.

Twenty-four Hours and Two Eyeballs

When this chapter was being written, business was booming at Google. Revenues had topped $10.6 billion for 2006. That was up 73 percent from 2005. This is the kind of growth many investors are willing to pay a lot of money for. Buffett, however, knows that no large-cap company, not even Google, can possibly continue growing at such a fantastic rate forever. In fact, while still impressive, Google's growth is already slowing. Revenue growth in 2005 was 93 percent. It was 118 percent in 2004. No one knows exactly when it will happen or by how much, but you can bet your life that growth will continue to slow until it reaches some sustainable level. After all, if it does not, Google will eventually end up owning all of the assets in the world!

As for The Washington Post, its revenues were only $3.8 billion in 2006, up only 10 percent from the prior year. The Post's expected growth rate is much lower than Google's, yet it is a rate that can be realistically sustained for many years. Compared to Google, expectations for the Post are reasonable. They have not gotten out of hand. Indeed, these reasonable expectations and realistic growth rates are part of what makes the Post the kind of stock that captures Buffett's attention. Of course, this does not necessarily mean that Buffett would be willing to buy more shares of the Post at the current price. On the contrary, he probably would not. After all, the Post, and the entire newspaper industry, has some real problems. Furthermore, Buffett is in the habit of buying stocks when they are cheap, not when they are fairly valued. However, at current valuations, Buffett obviously feels much more comfortable owning the Post than he does buying Google.

There is no question that Google is a great company with an extremely promising future. It is indeed shaking up the media industry and giving traditional companies like the Post a serious run for their money. Both daily and Sunday circulation at the Post are down almost 20 percent over the past ten years. Buffett himself said in a December 2006 CNBC interview that the newspaper industry is going downhill largely because of the Internet. Buffett pointed out that readers have only twenty-four hours a day and two eyeballs.[1]

Despite his well-publicized aversion to technology, Buffett would most likely agree that Google is a wonderful company. Yet great companies do not always make great stocks. Successful investors recognize the difference. If you are investing for the long run, you are always better off buying great companies. But you can end up with very mediocre returns, or even losses, if you pay too much. Buffett is the master of buying great companies at great prices. Perhaps someday he may even consider buying some shares of Google. But don't hold your breath. Google will have to get a whole lot cheaper before it shows up on Buffett's radar screen.

Just as stocks can get seriously overvalued when things are going well, Buffett knows that when things are going badly for a company many investors quickly give up hope. It is common, for example, to see a stock's price sink like a stone simply because earnings one quarter fell a few pennies shy of the consensus estimate. Without exercising much rational thought, investors simply assume the bad times will continue indefinitely. They often react impulsively by dumping the stock. Professional traders know this kind of reaction is likely to occur. That is why they, too, quickly dump the stock. They might even go further and short the stock. All this selling pressure can cause the stock's price to fall much lower than the fundamentals would justify.

Buffett recognizes that reactions of this kind can sometimes become ridiculously overdone. They frequently present excellent buying opportunities that can pay off big for patient investors. Of course, a plunge in price by itself is not enough to justify buying a stock. Many companies go bankrupt soon after the stock price collapses. Buffett would never blindly buy a stock simply because it was suddenly selling for a much lower price. But assuming the business is sound, there is no question that the reduced price invites further investigation.

Just a few short years after Google went public, investors had bid the stock price so high, the company's market capitalization eventually topped $200 billion. That dwarfed The Washington Post's $7.6 billion market cap at the time. Indeed, Google quickly became one of the largest publicly traded companies in America. Its market cap suddenly exceeded that of many well-known behemoths, including Intel, Coca-Cola, Goldman Sachs, and Merck. Google even rivals Berkshire Hathaway itself. Berkshire remained one of only a handful of publicly traded companies that was as large as or larger than Google.

Of course, it would be entirely misleading to compare Google to Berkshire by market cap alone. After all, market cap simply equals the stock price multiplied by the number of shares outstanding. As we saw earlier when comparing Google's valuation to that of The Washington Post, price does not mean much unless it is put in perspective. To properly compare Google to Berkshire, we need to transform the stock prices of both companies in some meaningful way.

As mentioned earlier in this chapter, one appropriate way to compare two stocks is to look at their market values relative to their book values. Book value is an accounting figure. In simple terms, it is the difference between net tangible assets and liabilities. It also tells us how much money shareholders have directly invested in the company plus the amount of money the company has retained over the years. In theory, book value is what should be left over if the company were to sell all of its assets for what they are valued on the balance sheet, and then paid off all of its liabilities.

Buffett has done a tremendous job of growing Berkshire's book value. At the end of 2006, it stood at $108 billion. In comparison, Google's book value was a relatively paltry $17 billion. Using more recent figures, Berkshire's market cap was just 1.6 times larger than its book value. Yet at the same time, Google's market cap was 9.0 times larger than its book value. Looking at these companies from this perspective, it becomes abundantly clear that Google is a much more expensive stock than Berkshire, even though each share of Berkshire Class A common stock was selling for about $120,000. Many investors would find this a little unusual, to say the least. After all, Berkshire has the wise and experienced team of Warren Buffett and Charlie Munger at the helm. Yet investors were obviously willing to pay a whole lot more for Google, a company founded by two technology geeks who just a few years earlier had dropped out of graduate school. Why? Simply because investors believed that Google could grow its business at a much faster rate than Berkshire.

Compared to Google, both Berkshire and The Washington Post appear bargain priced. As mentioned earlier, Berkshire has owned shares of the Post for more than three decades. Also, as previously mentioned, Berkshire owns no shares of Google. Buffett may not be willing to buy more shares of the Post at its recent price, but you can bet he is not going to jump into Google at its recent valuation either. Buffett knows that there is simply too much euphoria over Google. When investors flock to a stock like Google because they fall in love with the technology or get excited about just-reported financial results, the stock's price can go way too high for Buffett's taste. On the other hand, when investors shun a stock because they think the business is boring, or because the company missed earnings expectations, Buffett starts to get interested. Indeed, there are many companies in Berkshire's portfolio that were once troubled and out of favor. That was when Buffett first started buying them. Buffett's real success comes from buying companies just when everyone else thinks they have no potential for growth.

Gunslingers Versus Wise Elders

Stereotypes are often misleading, yet it is interesting to take a look at how the media portray growth and value investors. Growth investors are often presented as very aggressive. They are likened to gunslingers of the Old West—quick on the draw. They jump in and out of stocks without giving much thought to their actions. This is not always the case, of course. But it is a rather common stereotype.

Warren Buffett is believed to be a value investor, and value investors are usually portrayed as smart and savvy. They are thought to be like the wise elders of an ancient tribe. They do not rush to judgment. They do not make rash decisions. Instead, they are praised for exercising tremendous patience. They take plenty of time to study a company before committing any money—even if that means missing out on a rock-bottom price. After all, value investors buy for the long term, and long-term investors are in no particular hurry to part with their cash. They want to be very sure about their investment decisions.

Think of investors as drivers on a highway. Suppose there is a heavy traffic jam. "Growth" drivers become easily agitated. They get anxious. They start cursing and yelling. Their blood pressure goes up. They can't just sit there and do nothing. They have an unstoppable urge to take some action. Unfortunately, they sometimes end up doing something stupid. For example, they might suddenly start changing lanes. They might weave in and out of traffic. Often without realizing it, they will risk causing a serious accident. They end up putting a lot of wear and tear on their vehicle and a tremendous amount of stress on themselves, their passengers, and other drivers.

"Value" drivers know they are in the same situation as everyone else, but they react in a very different manner. First of all, they remain calm. They are smart enough to know there is no use getting upset. They also know it usually is not worth changing lanes too frequently. That does not mean they are not willing to consider alternatives. Indeed, they would be very happy to find a better way to get to their destination. Perhaps they have a map available, or better yet, a GPS navigation system that can direct them to an alternate route on a less-traveled road. While everyone is headed in one direction, they might take the nearest exit and go off in a different direction. They may end up driving a few extra miles, but they reach their final destination in a reasonable amount of time and with a whole lot less stress. If Buffett were stuck in traffic, chances are he would be a "value" driver.

Indeed, because of their tendency to go against the crowd, value investors are sometimes called "contrarians." They often buy the kinds of stocks others are selling, and sell those that others are buying. Although Buffett does not like to sell, neither does he chase the same stocks everyone else is after. He believes the less attention a stock attracts, the more likely it is to be reasonably priced. Buffett prefers to take the road less traveled.

Buffett Likes Undervalued Stocks Best

Warren Buffett is one of the richest men in the world. But he has garnered a reputation for being cheap. He was once asked why he wears such cheap suits. As he often does, he responded with humor, assuring his questioner that his suits are not cheap even though they may look cheap on him.

Although he can afford to buy anything he wants, Buffett prefers to lead a modest life. He drives a modest car and lives in the same relatively modest house he bought decades ago. But his reputation for being cheap is undeserved. Buffett certainly appreciates value, but he is not cheap. As a smart consumer and a smart investor, he knows there is often a big difference between price and value. Just because something is cheap does not mean it provides good value. On the other hand, value can sometimes be found in an item that appears expensive. Just as Buffett looks for value when he is shopping for a car with his own money, he looks for value when he is shopping for stocks with Berkshire's cash.

This certainly makes a lot of sense, but not everyone behaves this way. Those who do are not easily taken advantage of. They often find great bargains. When you go shopping for a new suit, would you not rather pay as little as possible? If you know one store is selling the same suit for $100 less than another store, would you not be willing to go at least a little out of your way to save some money? The same is true with investing. It is always best to pay as little as you can when buying any asset. But just as Buffett does not buy cheap suits, he is not going to buy a stock simply because it has a low price. He understands that sometimes it makes more sense to pay a premium for a stock with better prospects, even if that premium makes the stock appear expensive. The point is that while it may be true that Buffett has a general preference for value stocks over growth stocks, what he is really looking for is stocks that are undervalued.

This may sound like a rather subtle and unimportant difference, but it is critical to understanding Buffett's investment philosophy. Never confuse a value stock with an undervalued stock. As explained earlier in this chapter, a value stock is traditionally defined as one that has low price multiples. An undervalued stock, on the other hand, is one that is selling for less than it is worth. A value stock might be undervalued, but it could be overvalued. Likewise, a growth stock could be under- or overvalued. The point is that it is not important which category, value or growth, a stock falls into. The only thing that really matters is whether the stock is selling for more or less than it is worth. This happens because the market does not always properly price stocks.

As we saw in chapter 1, when it comes to diversification, Buffett does not entirely agree with finance theory. Diversification is not the only area where Buffett's views differ from the accepted norm. Here is another: Researchers and many experienced investors like to believe that stock markets are efficient. The word "efficient" has a very special connotation in the investing world.

An efficient market is one in which security prices react quickly to reflect all information. Academics talk about three forms of efficiency, depending on exactly what kind of information is being considered. These three forms are called weak, semistrong, and strong. Without complicating matters too much, it is sufficient for our purposes to know that if markets are truly efficient, as the theory dictates, then stocks are correctly priced—at least on average. In other words, in an efficient market, investors can be confident that the actual market price of a stock is an accurate reflection of what that stock is really worth. An important implication of this efficient market theory, or EMT, is that if stocks are correctly priced, one would not be able to consistently earn abnormal profits by trying to identify and purchase undervalued stocks. In fact, engaging in this kind of exercise would be a complete waste of time. As a result, those who are convinced that markets are efficient advise investors to stop trying to beat the market. Instead, they tell them to simply invest their money in index funds.

Buffett, however, specializes in finding undervalued stocks. His track record proves that it can be done. He has been able to do it successfully and consistently over a very long time. If the theory were correct, Buffett could not possibly have become as wealthy as he has. Therefore, based on Buffett's investment returns alone, one would have to conclude that either the man is somehow an exception to the rule, or there is no merit to the rule.

There is no question that Buffett is a truly exceptional investor. But he is not the only one to have produced market-beating returns on a consistent basis over long periods of time. There have been a sufficient number of other outstanding investors, including Peter Lynch, and Philip Fisher, to raise serious doubts about the merits of the EMT. Buffett himself cites Walter Schloss, another Benjamin Graham protégé, as a prime example of an outstanding investor. Schloss ran an investment partnership that significantly outperformed the benchmarks over almost fifty years. Buffett says, "There is simply *no* possibility that what Walter achieved over forty-seven years was due to chance."[2] Buffett goes on to castigate the academic community for its stubborn adherence to the EMT. Using one of his wonderful analogies, he adds, "Typically, a finance professor who had the nerve to question EMT had about as much chance of major promotion as Galileo had of being named Pope."[3]

Buffett's Secret Weapon

Since the evidence proves that Buffett and at least several others have been able to successfully and consistently beat the market by finding undervalued stocks, is it reasonable to assume that all investors can do the same thing? The bad news is that the answer is no. While it is possible for some investors to beat the market, it is impossible for all investors to do so. After all, on average, investors as a whole must earn the average return. That means some investors will do better, but others must do worse. This is exactly why many experts advocate an indexing approach. Buying an index fund is really the only way you can be certain to earn the market return.

The good news, however, is that *you* don't have to settle for average returns. You can improve your odds of being in the group that consistently beats the market. Like Buffett, you can do this by purchasing only the undervalued stocks and avoiding the ones that are overvalued. How can you tell if a stock is under- or overvalued? The only theoretically correct way is to conduct a *discounted cash flow* (DCF) analysis. Here is one area where Buffett agrees with the theory. Buffett finds undervalued stocks using this DCF approach.

Fortunately, conducting a DCF analysis is not easy. This is fortunate because if it were an easy thing to do, everyone would do it. And if everyone did it, there would be no advantage to doing it. Those who are willing to apply themselves and learn how to conduct a proper DCF analysis give themselves a distinct advantage over those who do not want to bother to learn the technique. Honing this skill requires a significant amount of study and practice. It is the foundation of security analysis. It is covered in all good college-level finance textbooks, and candidates studying for the Chartered Financial Analyst (CFA) designation are required to learn the methodology. It is also one of Buffett's favorite ways to spot undervalued stocks.

Some readers may be surprised to learn that Buffett relies on a methodology that appears to be somewhat complicated. After all, this is not consistent with his reputation for preferring things that are simple and easy to understand. However, people often forget that Buffett has the intellectual capability to tackle the most difficult problems. He is as skilled as any of the highly educated financial analysts found on Wall Street. In fact, he too has a first-rate business education. After spending two years at the University of Pennsylvania, he transferred to and graduated from the University of Nebraska in Lincoln. Then he earned a graduate degree from Columbia, where he studied under Benjamin Graham, one of the greatest investing experts of all time.

The specifics of this kind of analysis are beyond the scope of this book. Yet a cursory explanation of the DCF methodology is extremely useful for understanding and appreciating Buffett's way of thinking. Those who want to learn more are encouraged to acquire a copy of any one of the many outstanding college-level finance textbooks, for example, *Foundations of Finance: The Logic and Practice of Financial Management* (6th Edition) by Arthur J. Keown, John D. Martin, and John W. Petty (Prentice-Hall, 2007).

Discounting Cash Flows

DCF analysis is predicated on the premise that a share of stock must be worth the present value of all the future cash flows it is expected to generate for the investor. Every analyst, including Buffett, begins by estimating what those future cash flows will be. As you can imagine, there is tremendous potential for error. It is difficult enough to estimate what cash flows will be a year from now, let alone ten or twenty years down the road. Furthermore, there is no obvious right or wrong answer. One analyst's guess is as good as another's. Only time will tell which was right.

In order to estimate what those cash flows will be, the analyst must make assumptions about revenue growth rates, depreciation, capital expenditures, changes in working capital, profit margins, interest payments, taxes, and other factors. Obviously, the more items that have to be estimated, the greater the potential for error. The ability to make good projections is what distinguishes one analyst from another. Buffett excels at this game.

Once the projected cash flows are estimated, they have to be discounted back to the present in order to determine what they are worth in current dollars. Discounting is necessary because of the time value of money. In other words, a dollar today is worth more than a dollar tomorrow; and it is certainly worth much more than a dollar ten years from today. After all, if you lend someone money today, would you not prefer to get paid back as soon as possible? If you will not be repaid for several years, would you not expect to receive some return on the loan?

Discounting is the opposite of compounding. Instead of trying to determine how much an amount of money today will be worth in the future, we are trying to determine how much a future amount of money is worth today. For example, to find out how much $100 will be worth in five years if it earns 8 percent interest, we have to compound. But if we want to know how much $147 five years in the future is worth today, we have to discount. That discounted value is called the *present value,* or *intrinsic value.* One very important property of this discounting process is that intrinsic value is inversely related to the discount rate. In other words, the greater the interest rate that is used to discount the future cash flows, the smaller will be the intrinsic value of those cash flows.

The discount rate itself is a function of the general level of interest rates in the economy and the risk of an investment. When interest rates are high, or when the potential investment poses a lot of risk, a higher discount rate should be used. A high-risk investment is worth making in a high-interest-rate environment only if it can be purchased at a very good price. These are concepts Buffett understands intuitively. He also knows that sometimes the price is not low enough to justify making the investment. If this is the case, he simply does not buy.

DCF analysis can be used to value any asset, including stocks, bonds, and real estate. Many investors find it easy to understand how the process can be applied to bonds, since bonds typically make regular interest payments. Those interest payments are the bond's cash flows. For example, suppose you are considering buying a $1,000 par bond with a 10 percent coupon rate that matures in five years. If you buy the bond today, you will receive $100 a year for each of the next five years. In addition, in the fifth year, you will receive the $1,000 par value. How much is this bond worth today?

Using Buffett's favorite valuation methodology, the answer is derived by discounting all those future expected cash flows to the present. Before we can begin, however, we need to determine what discount rate to use. Remember that the discount rate is an interest rate that reflects not only current market rates, but also the risk of the bond. Suppose market interest rates are lower today than they were when the bond was first issued, so that the appropriate discount rate is 8 percent. The DCF process can be done automatically by plugging all the relevant figures into any standard financial calculator. It turns out the bond's intrinsic value is $1,079.85. If you could buy the bond for exactly this amount, you would earn an 8 percent annualized return on your investment. However, if the bond were selling in the market for $1,100, you should not buy it because it is overpriced. If you did pay $1,100 for the bond, you would earn less than 8 percent. On the other hand, if the bond were selling for $1,050, it would be underpriced. If you bought it for $1,050, you would earn more than an 8 percent return.

The process is simple enough for bonds. However, conducting

a DCF analysis on a stock is a lot more complicated because estimating the projected cash flows is not as straightforward. As we learned earlier, many assumptions must be made, and one analyst's guess is as good as another's. A bond's future expected cash flows are somewhat certain and easy to determine. But there is nothing certain about the cash flows from a stock.

Because Buffett has a propensity to buy stocks that pay dividends, investors often wonder if only the dividends should be discounted to determine the stock's intrinsic value. There is a dividend discount model that can be used for valuing stocks that have a significant and steadily growing payout. But this model is of no use when trying to value a company that does not pay dividends. Ironically, some investors insist that they would not buy stocks that do not pay dividends, yet in the same breath they will tell you that they would not hesitate to buy Berkshire Hathaway. Obviously, they do not realize that Berkshire pays no dividends. Although Buffett prefers to buy stocks that pay steadily growing dividends, he has kept Berkshire's payout at exactly zero. Despite the fact that Berkshire pays absolutely no dividends, the Class A stock was recently trading at close to $120,000 per share.[4]

The point is that there is more to cash flows than dividends. The cash flows do not actually have to be paid out to the investors to be included in a DCF analysis. The shareholders have rights to the cash flows whether or not they actually receive them. These cash flows might be reinvested in the company, but technically they belong to the shareholders. Therefore, a proper DCF analysis must include all the cash flows, whether they are paid out to investors or retained within the company and reinvested.

Recall that the most difficult part of conducting a DCF analysis involves making the cash flow projections. The actual discounting process is easily done using an electronic spreadsheet or a financial calculator. But projecting the cash flows requires making numerous assumptions and estimations. As a result, there is much room for error. Analysts soon learn that conducting a proper DCF analysis is as much art as it is science. Even projections made by analysts with many years of experience can turn out to be way off the mark. However, Buffett relies on this methodology because he knows that it is the only theoretically correct way to determine what a stock is worth.

Buffett Likes Simple Companies

Despite his reliance on DCF, Buffett recognizes the tremendous potential for error. He knows that when conducting a DCF analysis, no two analysts will derive exactly the same intrinsic value for a stock. Their estimates might not even be close. One might conclude the stock is undervalued, while the other determines it is overvalued. Buffett says, "Two people looking at the same set of facts, moreover—and that includes Charlie [Munger] and me—will almost inevitably come up with at least slightly different intrinsic value figures."[5] Unless the analysts use the same model and make the same assumptions, they will never get the same results. This is what creates a market for a stock. Both buyers and sellers have confidence in their respective analyses. Buyers think the stock is undervalued. Sellers think it is overvalued.

Buffett is frequently said to prefer companies that are easy to understand. Some have interpreted this to mean that he does not like to invest in complicated technology companies. There is certainly some truth to this, but what it really means is that Buffett prefers to avoid companies whose cash flows are difficult to project. An insurance company with a long history of steadily increasing cash flows is much easier to model than a technology company that recently went public and might not yet be profitable, even if it has promising and innovative products that might be a big hit someday. This is the real reason why Buffett has long avoided the technology sector.

Unfortunately, Buffett and his shareholders missed out on the great 1990s boom in technology stocks. Non-tech stocks had fallen so out of favor that investors even avoided shares of Berkshire Hathaway. Buffett's decision to avoid technology cost his shareholders dearly, as Berkshire's stock price fell by almost one half in just over a year. But the stock staged a recovery as soon as the prolonged bear market began. Berkshire was suddenly seen as a safe haven. Although Buffett and his shareholders missed out on the technology boom, they also avoided the ensuing crash.

Buffett likes to control risk. He does this primarily by avoiding companies if he thinks there is too much uncertainty about their future cash flows. Furthermore, because he believes there is little risk in buying companies that have predictable cash flows, he feels comfortable using the so-called risk-free rate to discount their projected cash flows. More specifically, he starts with the yield on U.S. Treasury bonds and makes some adjustments to it. A more conservative approach would argue for the use of a higher rate—in particular, one that properly reflects the stock's market-related risk. Buffett believes he does not need to account for risk in the discount rate since he consciously avoids stocks that he considers too risky.

Analysts and academics have criticized Buffett for this. They say that by using a discount rate that does not properly reflect risk, he is more likely to erroneously conclude that an overvalued stock is undervalued. Furthermore, by ignoring companies whose cash flows are difficult to understand, he is likely to miss out on great investment opportunities. Buffett stands guilty as charged, yet his track record speaks for itself.

Buffett Buys Stocks Cheap, Not Cheap Stocks

Warren Buffett does not buy cheap stocks. The secret to his success lies in his knack for buying stocks cheap. He relies on DCF analysis to find these stocks. He uses DCF analysis to determine the stock's intrinsic value, which he compares to the market price. Buffett wants to buy only if the intrinsic value is greater than the market price. If it is less, he is not interested.

Of course, Buffett does not sit around analyzing every stock that comes along. For example, earlier in this chapter, we concluded that Google looks quite expensive when its price multiples are compared to those of The Washington Post and Berkshire. But a DCF analysis is the best way to determine if Google is really overvalued. Buffett has never bought Google. Could it be that he conducted a DCF analysis on Google and concluded it was overvalued? Probably not. Buffett would likely argue that Google's cash flows are too difficult to project with any degree of confidence. He would rather spend his time analyzing companies he understands. In other words, he would rather focus on companies whose cash flows can be projected with a greater degree of certainty.

Yet even when Buffett finds a stock that is undervalued, he knows there is no guarantee about when the price will rise. It may rise quickly, or it may never go up. This is where great patience is a real virtue. When Buffett buys a stock he believes is undervalued, he is betting that other investors will eventually come around to his way of thinking. He is betting that they too will wake up someday and realize the stock is undervalued. He is betting that they will begin to buy the stock and bid up its price until it is correctly valued. Of course, this is no sure bet. Yet Buffett knows that he is more likely to make money in the long run by consistently buying undervalued stocks than by consistently buying stocks that are overvalued. Buffett knows that investing is a game of probabilities. By buying only undervalued stocks he is stacking the odds in his favor.

So it is not correct to conclude that Warren Buffett is a value investor. He may have a general preference for value stocks over growth stocks, but only because value stocks are more likely than growth stocks to be undervalued. It would really be more accurate to call Buffett an "undervalued" investor. The point is that when he says he likes to buy cheap stocks, he is not talking about price multiples. Instead, he is talking about discounting cash flows to find stocks with intrinsic values that are greater than what he would have to pay for them in the market. Thus, Buffett is not really looking to buy cheap stocks at all. Instead, he is looking to buy stocks cheap.

KEY TAKEAWAYS: CHAPTER 2

- Value stocks are traditionally defined as those stocks with low price multiples. Growth stocks are those having high price multiples. Buffett is widely believed to be a strict value investor. This is a myth. Many of the companies he has purchased over the years on Berkshire's behalf have exhibited tremendous growth. *It is always best to pay as little as possible for any stock. However, high-growth companies are worth more than low-growth companies. Therefore, it makes perfect sense to pay a premium for expected growth. Do not avoid growth stocks simply because they sell for higher multiples.*

- Buffett is willing to buy growth stocks, but he is also aware that investors' expectations can get out of hand. Investors tend to extrapolate recent events into the future. As a result, they sometimes bid up the price of high-growth stocks too much, causing them to become seriously overvalued. Alternatively, they may shun companies with disappointing growth, driving their prices down to extremely attractive levels. *Although you should be willing to pay up for growth, it is extremely important not to pay too much. Also, do not overlook low-growth companies that are selling at ridiculously low prices because investors have given up on them. The key to long-term investment success lies in being able to buy great companies at great prices.*

- Successful investors must be able to distinguish between great companies and great stocks. Google is a great company. It is dominating the Internet space. The Washington Post, which used to be a great company, is now struggling with declining newspaper circulation. *When it comes to stocks, price is the only thing that matters. A company may be great for a number of reasons, but a stock is great only if it is selling for less than it is worth. Buying great companies is generally a good idea, but successful investors know it is more important to buy great stocks. Learn to focus on price even if you plan to hold for the long term.*

- Academics often argue that markets are efficient. Buffett knows this is not the case. There are too many anomalies and too many successful investors to assume markets are efficient. *Do not make the mistake of assuming the markets are always right. If you are a skilled investor, you should stay alert for opportunities to buy stocks when they are obviously undervalued.*

- Buffett has a penchant for value, but what he really seeks are "undervalued" companies. Like most good financial analysts, Buffett relies on a discounted cash flow (DCF) methodology to identify a company's intrinsic value, which he then compares to the price he would have to pay to buy the business. *The best way to find underpriced stocks is to discount projected cash flows and compare the resulting intrinsic value to the market price. You should focus your efforts on buying undervalued stocks, not value stocks.*

- Analysts spend years learning how to conduct a DCF analysis, yet the process is as much art as it is science. Because it requires making forecasts about the future, no two analysts will arrive at exactly the same conclusion. *Practice makes perfect. A good way to start is by getting your hands on some sell-side research reports and looking at the DCF models. Try to decide where the analyst's assumptions might be too aggressive or too conservative. You should have more confidence that a stock is undervalued if the assumptions seem too conservative.*

3

Value for the Long Run, Growth for the Short

The trend is your friend.

Don't confuse brains with a bull market.

—Two popular Wall Street adages

We learned in chapter 2 that Warren Buffett loves undervalued stocks. He relies heavily on DCF analysis to find them. He computes intrinsic values and focuses his attention on those companies and stocks that can be purchased for less. Buffett has a propensity for value stocks because value stocks are more likely than growth stocks to be undervalued. So if he had to choose strictly between value and growth, he would be much more likely to go with value. He knows that, based on fundamentals alone, growth stocks are often overvalued. Investors love to chase after growth. Because growth stocks are so popular, their prices can get too high to justify purchase by long-term buy-and-hold investors like Buffett. Value stocks, however, often go unloved. Because there is less interest in these stocks, astute investors can often purchase value stocks at prices that are well below intrinsic value.

The point is that even though growth stocks can sometimes be undervalued as determined by a DCF analysis, there is a greater chance that value stocks will be undervalued. Therefore, if conducting a complicated DCF analysis is not your cup of tea, you would not be straying too far off the Buffett path if you focused your energies on low-multiple value stocks.

But is it really possible to outperform the market by following a strict value strategy? Although Berkshire Hathaway's investment strategy is not strictly value, it certainly is more value oriented than growth oriented. And shares of Berkshire have appreciated more than 20 percent annually for several decades. Clearly, a value bent has paid off handsomely for Buffett and his fellow Berkshire shareholders. Berkshire's performance has truly been outstanding, but that's just one example. Is there any other compelling evidence that a value-oriented investment strategy is better than one focused on growth?

The answer is yes. Value consistently beats growth—but only in the long run. Indeed, to be a successful value investor, you have to have the patience of, well, Warren Buffett. Buffett frequently stresses the virtues of long-term investing. He frowns on short-term trading. Buffett is not interested in making a quick buck. He knows that value investing does not make one wealthy overnight. If that is what you are looking for, you will be sadly disappointed. To be a successful value investor, you should have a target holding period of at least five years, preferably longer. Indeed, the longer you are willing to wait, the greater the odds that a value strategy will work well for you.

Seven Times Your Money in Ten Years

Figure 3.1 is derived from data published in a well-known academic study conducted by Eugene Fama and Kenneth French.[1] The authors examined the long-run performance of value stocks and growth stocks. First they took all the stocks on the New York Stock Exchange, the American Stock Exchange, and the NASDAQ for which they could get reliable data. Then they divided them into ten groups based on their price-to-book (P-B) ratios. (Actually, the authors used the book-to-price ratio, which is simply the reciprocal of the price-to-book ratio.) Group 1 consists of the most extreme value stocks. Group 10 contains the most extreme growth stocks.

Figure 3.1

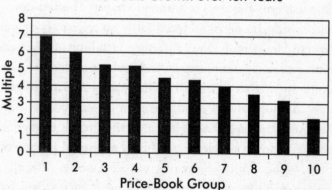

Value Beats Growth over Ten Years

Group 1 contains the stocks with the lowest price-book ratios. Group 10 contains the stocks with the highest price-book ratios. Group 1 stocks went up almost seven times in value over ten years. Group 10 stocks did only slightly better than a double. *(Source: Fama and French)*

Fama and French analyzed a twenty-seven-year period that includes both bull and bear markets. They calculated average monthly returns for each group, and what they found was nothing short of spectacular. Value stocks significantly outperformed growth stocks. On average, the most extreme value stocks—those in Group 1—went up almost seven times in price in ten years. That comes out to about a 21 percent annualized rate of return. Coincidentally, that is very close to Berkshire's actual long-term performance. However, the most extreme growth stocks—those in Group 10—only about doubled in price in ten years. That comes out to a comparatively disappointing annualized return of just under 8 percent.

According to these results, Buffett, who often relies on instinct and common sense, was right all along. Long-term investors should focus on value, not growth.

Of course, Fama and French's methodology is not exactly comparable to Buffett's investment strategy. Buffett does not make investment decisions based solely on price-to-book multiples. He considers all kinds of factors, including intrinsic value, return on equity, profit margins, and, perhaps most important for him (as we shall see in chapter 5), the quality of management.

In addition, when Buffett makes an investment, he tends to hold for a very long time. The Fama and French methodology does not follow a simple buy-and-hold approach. It actually requires a good deal of monitoring and rebalancing. After all, this year's value stock could be next year's growth stock, in which case it would fall out of one group and into another. But Buffett does not constantly rebalance his portfolio like this. He does not kick out one stock and purchase another simply because their prices and multiples have changed. With some exceptions, when Buffett buys a stock, he sticks with it for the very long term. This is true if the price unexpectedly falls and also if the price appreciates much faster than he initially anticipated. In fact, as we will learn in chapter 4, Buffett likes to think in terms of buying businesses, not stocks. If you owned a business, perhaps you would consider selling it simply because you could get a great price. Buffett, however, would not. Buffett loves to buy. Selling does not come as naturally to him.

What's the Matter with Italy?

For years Buffett had little or no interest in international markets. He focused solely on U.S. companies and stocks. In recent periods, however, he has been paying some attention to other parts of the world as well. For example, he bought Iscar Metalworking, an Israeli company (discussed in chapter 5), in 2006. He also bought shares of PetroChina. (Buffett, however, sold PetroChina in 2007.) Given Buffett's growing interest in investing abroad, it is reasonable to ask if value beats growth everywhere or just in the United States.

Fortunately, Fama and French wondered the same thing. They extended their study to include data from twelve major non-U.S. markets.[2] They examined a twenty-year period and, for the most part, what they found in other countries confirmed their earlier U.S. results. Value stocks outperformed growth stocks in eleven of those twelve non-U.S. markets. Italy, for some odd reason, was the only country to buck the trend. Warren Buffett's long-term value-oriented investment strategy appears to work well almost everywhere on the planet.

Value Is Good; Small-Cap Value Is Better

Berkshire Hathaway has produced outstanding returns for many decades. Buffett, however, has warned that Berkshire cannot possibly do as well in the future. This is because the company has grown much too big to keep performing in the same manner. Indeed, market observers have long noticed that growth usually slows when a company gets bigger. They have noticed that small companies often produce the biggest returns.

Fama and French's research has convinced many money managers that value beats growth over the long term. But the researchers also wanted to know if size matters as well. Is Buffett right to think that Berkshire is less likely to produce outstanding returns now that it has grown so large?

Just as they did previously, Fama and French took all the stocks for which they could get reliable data and put them into ten groups. But instead of dividing them up based on price-to-book ratios, this time they segmented the stocks based on market capitalization. Group 1 in Figure 3.2 includes the stocks with the smallest market caps. Group 10 includes those with the largest market caps. Average results for ten-year holding periods are displayed in the figure. The smallest-cap stocks went up almost six times in price over ten years. The largest-cap stocks did much worse. They did not even triple in price.

Figure 3.2

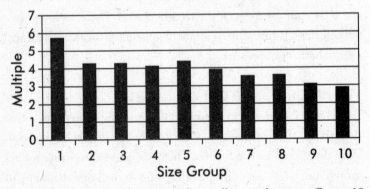

Small Beats Large over Ten Years

Group 1 contains the stocks with the smallest market caps. Group 10 contains the stocks with the largest market caps. Group 1 stocks went up almost six times in value over ten years. Group 10 stocks less than tripled in value over ten years. *(Source: Fama and French)*

As we learned in chapter 1, Buffett would urge most investors to diversify their portfolios extensively. He recommends they use index funds to do this. So for diversification purposes alone, Buffett would likely say that investors should own both small-cap and large-cap stocks. Of course, if they are truly diversified, they would also own both value stocks and growth stocks.

However, based on Fama and French's results, it is clear that long-term investors who want to maximize returns should tilt their portfolios toward small-cap value stocks. Buffett's penchant for value stocks is well known. Small-cap stocks, however, are not his usual thing. As much as he might like to own them, it is simply not realistic for him to do so. This is because Berkshire Hathaway has become such a huge conglomerate with such a vast amount of money to invest. It is really not feasible for Buffett to focus on small-cap companies and stocks. If he tried to, he would have to buy a tremendous number of them. While Buffett thinks extensive diversification is good for most investors, and while Berkshire is more diversified today than it has ever been, the fact remains that Buffett prefers to keep Berkshire's investments somewhat concentrated. To accomplish this, he must favor large companies and large-cap stocks. Given the amount of cash Buffett is working with, he really has no choice.

Buffett makes his preference for large-cap acquisitions perfectly clear each year in Berkshire's annual reports. This is stated in the section entitled "Acquisition Criteria." In May 2007, Buffett said he was looking to spend $40 to $60 billion on a single acquisition. Although Buffett's aversion to selling anything is well known, he even said at that time that he would consider selling something in order to help finance the purchase.

Traders Provide Liquidity

The results are convincing enough. Value beats growth, and small-cap value beats large-cap value. But this is true only on average, and only in the long term. Most research studies on the subject tend to define the long run as at least five years. Most professionals also think of the long run in the same way. Warren Buffett thinks more in terms of decades; and the longer the investment horizon, the more likely that value will outperform growth. Despite his obvious preference for value over growth, we have also seen that Buffett sometimes buys growth stocks. Buffett realizes that growth stocks can sometimes be undervalued on a discounted cash flow basis.

Furthermore, it turns out that growth stocks actually do better than value stocks over the short term. However, Buffett fans are likely disgusted by the very idea of short-term investing. Indeed, long-term value investors usually refuse even to refer to those who think about the short term as "investors." Instead, they prefer to call them "traders."

Warren Buffett is perhaps the most successful long-term, buy-and-hold investor, but he is not the only proponent of this investment strategy. Vanguard founder Jack Bogle is the most enthusiastic champion of long-term investing using index funds. Other successful investors who have taken a long-term perspective on the markets include Peter Lynch, who ran Fidelity's Magellan Fund for about a dozen years, and John Templeton, who founded the eponymous company currently called Franklin Templeton Investments.

Buffett says his favorite holding period is forever, yet even he has engaged in a number of relatively short-term trades. So why is it so wrong to think about the short term? After all, short-term investors, or traders, or whatever you want to call them, are not bad people. Like every other investor in the market, they are simply trying to make money. The only real difference, of course, is their intended holding period. Furthermore, the determined efforts of short-term traders to beat the market provide valuable liquidity that benefits even the long-term investors. Imagine what the markets would be like if everyone was a long-term investor. There would be very little volatility because there would be very little trading going on. If no one was willing to trade, Buffett and others who wanted to buy stocks for the long term would have difficulty finding sellers. If there were not enough sellers, it would be extremely difficult to invest long-term 401(k) or IRA money on a regular basis.

And what about those who want to sell? Buffett may not like to sell, but he does sell stocks from time to time. Many long-term investors need to sell stocks on a regular basis—especially after they retire—in order to generate the necessary funds to pay their bills. If there were not enough traders in the market who are willing to buy, long-term sellers would be out of luck. And if stocks do not trade for several weeks or even several days, how would we know what they are really worth? We could not have much confidence in quoted prices that are stale. How much value would your shares really hold if you could not quickly sell them when you wanted to?

So whatever Buffett may think personally of short-term investing as a viable strategy, he at least appreciates the valuable liquidity short-term traders provide to the market. Buffett knows liquidity benefits all investors. It also benefits corporations. After all, if investors were not able to buy and sell when they wanted to, corporations would face much higher financing costs.

Why Traders Prefer Growth

Recall that the traditional way of defining value or growth is to focus on price multiples. Stocks with low multiples are value stocks. Those with high multiples are growth stocks. But there are other ways to define growth. For example, a growth stock could be one that has a high rate of expected growth in sales or earnings. It might also have high price multiples, but not necessarily. Nonetheless, even when defined the traditional way, it turns out that growth stocks frequently exhibit *momentum.*

Now, there's a really loaded word. This is because value investors hate momentum investors even more than they hate growth investors. You can bet that Warren Buffett is not a fan of momentum investing. Perhaps he should be. After all, by refusing to engage in this time-tested investment strategy, he and his Berkshire shareholders missed out on some great opportunities during the 1990s technology boom.

Do not confuse momentum investing with day trading. Although both strategies rely on that old adage, "The trend is your friend," they are not the same thing. The major difference is that day traders are looking to make money in extremely short periods of time. They might hold a position in a stock for just a few hours—sometimes even less. Momentum investors look for good returns over longer holding periods. Admittedly, they do not have Buffett-like patience, but their typical holding period ranges from six to eighteen months. In many cases, it is long enough to allow them to take advantage of favorable long-term capital gains treatment.

While it is true that momentum investing is riskier than long-term value investing, and that it requires a higher degree of monitoring and a greater amount of trading, it is also true that there is compelling empirical evidence that using this strategy can be a profitable way to invest. One of the first serious momentum studies was conducted by Narasimhan Jegadeesh and Sheridan Titman.[3] These researchers found that investors could indeed generate considerable profits by shorting stocks that had done poorly over the prior six months and buying stocks that had been doing well during that same period. The resulting profits from this strategy cannot be explained by risk. Furthermore, the profits were large enough to cover transaction costs. It turns out that this momentum-based strategy works best for investment horizons of about twelve months. In fact, the researchers found that by twenty-four months, almost half the twelve-month profits had disappeared. (See Figure 3.3.)

Figure 3.3

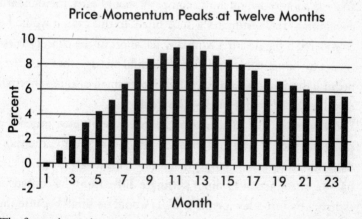

Price Momentum Peaks at Twelve Months

The figure shows the average cumulative returns for portfolios consisting of long positions and short positions. Long positions are in stocks that exhibited positive price momentum over the prior six months. Short positions are in stocks with negative price momentum. The strategy generates profits that peak in about twelve months' time. *(Source: Jegadeesh and Titman)*

A few years later, Jegadeesh teamed up with two other economists, Louis Chan and Josef Lakonishok, and published another and more comprehensive momentum study in the same journal.[4] One of their more interesting findings was that the stocks that did the best according to this momentum strategy were also the ones that traditionalists define as growth stocks. In other words, the best-performing stocks were the ones with the highest price-to-book ratios. It turns out they were also the ones with the largest SUEs.

SUE is an acronym that stands for *standardized unexpected earnings*. It is an ingenious way to determine how much importance investors should assign to earnings surprises. SUE is defined as the difference between a company's actual earnings per share and the consensus estimate divided by the standard deviation of all the analysts' estimates. If there is a lot of agreement among the analysts about how much the company should earn, the standard deviation of their estimates will be small. In this case, it would be considered a big deal if a company fell short of the consensus estimate by just a penny or two. SUE would be large (but negative) because the denominator is small. A rather small earnings shortfall could result in a big sell-off in the stock.

Alternatively, if the analysts cannot agree on how much the company should earn and their estimates vary greatly, the standard deviation will be large. When this happens, it is not such a big surprise if actual earnings per share differ from the consensus estimate by just a few pennies. SUE would be small because the denominator is large. The stock price should not react as violently.

Many investors are not familiar with SUE because it is not typically available on the financial Web sites they frequent. However, professional investors love this measure and are willing to pay good money for data feeds that provide it.

No doubt Warren Buffett knows all about SUE, too. However, Buffett has been extremely critical of measures that focus attention on quarterly earnings. He thinks managers already spend too much time thinking about short-term results and not enough time thinking strategically about the long term. As we will see in chapter 10, if it were up to Buffett, corporations would stop providing quarterly earnings guidance altogether.

Buffett may ignore it, but many professional investors pay a lot of attention to SUE. Interestingly, the academic evidence indicates that they are right to do so. The bottom line is that stocks exhibit momentum, and growth stocks with the largest SUEs exhibit the greatest momentum. However, like any investment strategy, including Buffett's, momentum investing works only on average. It most certainly does not work in every single instance. There is no question that Buffett's long-term buy-and-hold focus has paid off big for Berkshire Hathaway and its shareholders. Yet Buffett's way is not the only profitable way to invest. Indeed, Buffett's refusal to consider alternative strategies has at times resulted in missed opportunities.

Momentum Investing and the Dot-com Bubble

Day trading was quite popular during the late-1990s technology boom. But it quickly fell out of favor when the dot-com bubble burst and all kinds of stocks came crashing down. Of course, the technology sector, where most of the interest was at the time, was the biggest loser. No doubt this gave Buffett at least some measure of satisfaction. After all, he had been strongly criticized by some for missing out on the tech-led rally. But once the boom ended, his long-term value approach was once again in favor. In fact, shares of Berkshire Hathaway, which had been falling in 1999, began to rally again in 2000 just as the rest of the market went into a prolonged sell-off.

Many value investors were pleased to see the bursting of the dot-com bubble. After all, they had been saying all along, "Don't confuse brains with a bull market." Although momentum investing is not exactly the same thing as day trading, those who had been implementing momentum strategies in the late 1990s and had purchased high-growth stocks with large SUEs just before they fell out of favor incurred big losses. This should come as no surprise. After all, just like every investment strategy, momentum investing works only on average—not every time. Indeed, there is no perfect investment strategy. Even value investing does not come with a guarantee.

Despite those losses, do not judge momentum investing too harshly. You may be surprised to learn that a strict momentum strategy would have become profitable again soon after the bursting of the dot-com bubble began. This is because a few months into the sell-off, a momentum-based approach would have prompted the investor to short the very technology stocks that were plummeting. Because these stocks continued to fall through the end of 2002, profits earned from shorting them would have been substantial.

Nonetheless, there is no denying that momentum investing involves more work and exposes the investor to greater risks than Buffett's simple, long-term, buy-and-hold value approach. As mentioned earlier, momentum investing requires constant monitoring and a good amount of turnover. The greater turnover results in more frequent recognition of capital gains and the resulting tax liabilities that go with them. It also results in greater trading costs. Thanks to the Internet, however, trading costs these days can be kept quite low. The days of forking over $100 or more in commissions to a full-service broker just to execute a simple trade are over. Today, many online brokerage firms charge less than $10 for a trade almost regardless of the quantity of shares that are being bought or sold. One major firm even began advertising zero-commission trades.

To be sure, momentum investing is not for everyone. It certainly is not for Warren Buffett and it may not be appropriate for you. Yet it is wrong to believe that only value investors make money. It is also wrong to believe that value investing is always superior to other investment strategies, including a growth-oriented momentum approach. Value does beat growth over the long term, yet there is plenty of evidence that growth and momentum beat a buy-and-hold value-oriented strategy over shorter investment horizons.

Buffett's long-term value approach is easy to understand and even easier to implement. It requires very little work. You might even call it the lazy person's approach to investing. There is absolutely nothing wrong with this. Many investors prefer it. Those who follow a value strategy can simply buy a portfolio of stocks and head off to the beach or the golf course and actually enjoy their lives. Value investing can be very profitable indeed.

Yet momentum investing can also be quite profitable. It is not as easy to understand as value investment, and it is certainly more difficult to implement. It requires a lot more work. Unlike day trading, however, momentum investing does not force you to keep your eyes glued to a computer screen all day long.

Nonetheless, the best approach for you will depend on what you are trying to accomplish. If you are a patient investor with a long-term investment horizon and you prefer not to monitor your investments so often, Buffett's long-term value approach is the way to go. But if you want to see faster gains and can tolerate more risks, and if you are willing to devote a considerable amount of time to monitoring your investments, a growth-oriented momentum approach might make you happier. No matter which approach you choose, at the very least, you should be aware of what works—and what does not work—in the long run as well as the short run. Knowing only half the story can lead to unrealistic expectations. It can also get even the best-intentioned investor into plenty of hot water.

KEY TAKEAWAYS: CHAPTER 3

- Buffett is a long-term investor. If he had to choose strictly between value and growth, he would go with value. Empirical research proves he would be right to do so. Value stocks beat growth stocks over the long term. One study found that for ten-year holding periods, the most extreme value stocks outperformed the most extreme growth stocks by more than three times. *If you are a long-term buy-and-hold investor, tilt your portfolio toward value stocks and away from growth stocks.*

- Because Berkshire Hathaway has grown so large, Buffett is forced to favor large-cap companies and stocks. However, research shows that small-cap stocks outperform large-cap stocks over the long term. *Long-term buy-and-hold investors should tilt their portfolios toward small-cap stocks.*

- Empirical research also proves that stocks exhibit momentum. Those that have done well in the recent past tend to continue doing well in the near future. Those that have done poorly in the recent past tend to do poorly in the near future. Momentum appears to persist for about twelve months. Furthermore, growth stocks with the biggest earnings surprises exhibit the strongest amount of momentum. Buffett's refusal to consider momentum investing cost his shareholders dearly during the tech boom of the 1990s. Of course, it also insulated them from the ensuing sell-off that began in 2000. *Despite the long-run superiority of value over growth, it turns out that growth beats value over shorter investment horizons. Investors looking for outsized returns over shorter investment horizons should focus on growth stocks exhibiting strong momentum. They should realize, however, that this strategy also involves greater risks.*

- Buffett's long-term focus helps him minimize trading costs and taxes. Momentum investing requires more monitoring, more frequent trading, and results in greater taxes. *Those following a long-term buy-and-hold approach can spend more time enjoying their lives. Those favoring a momentum-based investment approach must work harder. They will also incur greater costs.*

4

Never Marry a Stock

Regardless of price, we have no interest at all in selling any good businesses that Berkshire owns. We are also very reluctant to sell sub-par businesses as long as we expect them to generate at least some cash and as long as we feel good about their managers and labor relations.

—Warren Buffett

When you ask investors about Warren Buffett, you will hear statements like "Buffett is a genius," and "Buffett is the greatest investor of all time." Eventually, someone will call him a great stock picker.

Buffett, however, would probably disagree—at least with the stock-picker part. This is not because his stock picks have not been great. Indeed, many have been outstanding. His objection also has nothing to do with his widely acknowledged humility. The real reason Buffett would disagree is because he simply does not believe that stock picking has much to do with investing. In fact, Buffett believes that true investing is more about buying businesses than it is about picking stocks.

Buffett Marries Businesses

Getting married is a major commitment. Love is a necessary condition to make a successful marriage, but love alone is not sufficient. Much more is needed. Before walking down the aisle, you should learn as much as possible about the one you intend to marry. Compatibility, trust, family, upbringing, religion, education, career, and financial condition all come into consideration. Marriage, after all, involves a long-term commitment. While there are no guarantees and you can never really be 100 percent certain, you should at least try to minimize the probability of making a wrong decision before tying the knot.

Furthermore, when you enter into a marriage you are not likely to walk out just because a prettier face happens to come along. You are not likely to call it quits just because you have some disagreements. Of course, if it becomes absolutely clear that there are irreconcilable differences, divorce is always an option. But divorce is messy and extremely expensive. It should never be taken lightly. It should be employed only as a last resort. Divorce should not be the first thing on your mind when you are seriously thinking about getting married.

In Warren Buffett's mind, buying a business is like getting married. One difference, of course, is that while he can have just one wife at a time, he can own as many businesses as he can afford. Yet in every case, when Buffett buys a business, he knows he is making a major commitment. This is why he tries to buy only good businesses that he plans to keep for the long run. All serious Buffett fans know this is part of his mystique.

In fact, Buffett frequently makes a distinction between buying businesses and simply buying stocks. He urges investors to think more like business buyers and less like stock traders. He also believes investors should stick with good businesses even when those businesses are struggling, just as they would stick with a good marriage through good times and bad. Similarly, Buffett says he will not sell a good business simply because he can fetch a price that is much greater than the intrinsic value. Perhaps most surprising of all, however, is his attitude about poor-performing businesses that he currently owns. He won't sink more money into them and he may regret having bought them, but he is also extremely reluctant to sell them. He states this very clearly as Principle #11 in Berkshire's "Owner's Manual" (found in every annual report):

> You should be fully aware of one attitude Charlie and I share that hurts our financial performance: Regardless of price, we have no interest at all in selling any good businesses that Berkshire owns. We are also very reluctant to sell sub-par businesses as long as we expect them to generate at least some cash and as long as we feel good about their managers and labor relations. We hope not to repeat the capital-allocation mistakes that led us into such sub-par businesses. And we react with great caution to suggestions that our poor businesses can be restored to satisfactory profitability by major capital expenditures. (The projections will be dazzling and the advocates sincere, but, in the end, major additional investment in a terrible industry usually is about as rewarding as struggling in quicksand.) Nevertheless, gin rummy managerial behavior (discard your least promising business at each turn) is not our style. We would rather have our overall results penalized a bit than engage in that kind of behavior.

This is fascinating stuff to investing experts because it is not considered rational. It is completely contrary to the idea of wealth maximization. A rational investor would be thrilled to sell something for more than it is worth. He would also be happy to get rid of something that is not producing an adequate return. The amazing thing is that Buffett is fully aware of this and openly admits that his policies are detrimental to his shareholders. Yet at the same time, there is perhaps no single individual in the history of investing who has done a better job than Warren Buffett of maximizing shareholder wealth over the long term.

What explains this seemingly irrational behavior? It is due largely to the distinction Buffett makes between buying businesses and buying stocks. Most investors do not really appreciate this critical difference. After all, it sounds a bit nonsensical. In order to own the business, you must buy the stock. Stock, after all, is referred to as equity. He who owns the equity owns the business.

Yet in Buffett's mind, the difference has to do with commitment. Buying a business involves a serious commitment. Buying stock requires very little commitment. Here is one way to appreciate the difference. If your investment in a business represents a major portion of your net worth, whether you are buying the entire company or just a small portion of it, you will be extremely focused and committed to the success of that business. On the other hand, if your ownership stake represents just a small fraction of your net worth, your level of commitment is not nearly the same. If you aren't happy with how things are going, you can simply take your losses and get out. You might even obtain a nice tax benefit when you sell.

Berkshire Hathaway has a habit of buying entire businesses— or at least very substantial chunks of businesses. Buffett is saying that even if you cannot afford to do the same, you should at least think of yourself as a business buyer rather than a stock buyer. You should realize that you are committing real capital; and before committing any capital, a business buyer would first do some research—what is often referred to in the investment industry as "due diligence." Furthermore, a smart business buyer is not likely to commit capital with the intention of flipping it in a short period of time. Indeed, Buffett says that when he makes an investment, he does not even think in terms of exit strategies.[1] Yet even those business buyers who have an explicit exit strategy in mind typically plan on sticking with their investment decision for at least a number of years.

Just as you would if you were getting married, before buying a business, you should learn as much as you possibly can about it. What products does it produce? What services does it provide? Who are its most important suppliers and customers? How large is the entire market? Is the market growing or is it stagnant? How big is the company's market share? Is the management team competent, trustworthy, and willing to stay on after the transaction? Who are the key employees? Are they talented, happy, and loyal to the company? Is the company financially stable, or does it have an excessive amount of debt that might put it in financial jeopardy if the company hits a rough patch? What are the key metrics in this company's industry? What do profit margins, return on equity, and book value look like?

These are the kinds of questions that go through Buffett's mind because when he makes an investment, he typically commits a very large amount of money. Buffett is in it for the long haul. The answers to these kinds of questions are not a matter of great consequence to those who are thinking about a quick trade, but they are critical to long-term investors. Just as in a marriage, business buyers are planning to tie a knot that cannot easily be undone.

When you make an investment and you are thinking like a business buyer, you realize you are becoming an owner in the true sense of the word. A business buyer (as opposed to a stock trader) is not going to cut and run just because earnings happen to fall short of expectations one quarter and the stock looks like it may tumble several points. Similarly, a business buyer is not going to sell and turn a quick profit just because the stock price suddenly leaps much higher and faster than initially expected. This is why Buffett says he won't sell a good business even if he can get more for it than it is worth, and why he won't sell an underperforming business as long as it is generating some return.

Most Investors Date Stocks

Dating is very different from marriage. You may think you are in love, but you are not really sure. You want to spend some time together, but you are not necessarily interested in a long-term relationship. You are willing to assume some responsibility, but you are not ready for a major commitment. Most important, you want to keep your options open just in case something better comes along. If you are just dating, it is a whole lot easier to break up if things don't work out. There is no messy and expensive divorce to deal with.

If business buyers think in terms of marriage, stock buyers think in terms of dating. In fact, there is an old adage on Wall Street: "Never marry a stock." Those who buy stocks always keep this adage in mind.

Stock buyers are not willing to make the kind of commitment

that business buyers make; and buying stocks, as opposed to buy-ing businesses, implies a certain amount of trading. Stock buyers also are not typically willing to risk a large amount of capital in any one position, and they most certainly are not thinking of holding their investment forever. Stock buyers are more than happy to sell if and when the right opportunity presents itself. Buffett may object, but the fact is that the average investor *must* think more like a stock buyer than a business buyer. After all, the average investor can afford to buy just a few hundred or a few thousand shares of any one company. That is not enough to give the investor the kind of influence a business buyer like Buffett enjoys. Furthermore, the average investor may not be in a position to ride out rough patches for very long.

When buying stocks rather than businesses, price is one of the foremost considerations. Obviously, it is best to buy low, but a stock buyer does not object to buying high and selling higher. All of the things that are really important when buying a business for the long term, such as market share, quality of management, profit margins, and return on equity, are not nearly as important when buying a stock for the shorter term. While it is always a good idea to become familiar with these fundamental factors, they are not going to make or break your investment decision.

A stock buyer knows that if a stock is selling for less than in-trinsic value, it becomes a clear candidate for purchase. Even Buf-fett would agree with this. However, those who buy stocks rather than businesses are also thinking about selling. Recall that Buffett has no exit strategy. To a stock buyer, however, getting out is as important as getting in. Stock buyers know that if stocks can be-come undervalued, they can also become overvalued. They know that if it makes sense to buy undervalued stocks, then it must also make sense to sell overvalued ones. Buffett knows this, too. But

Buffett prefers to get married. He does not like to sell. As we saw earlier in this chapter, Buffett says he will not sell a good business even if he can get more for it than it is worth. Those who buy stocks, however, are ready and willing to sell—especially when it becomes evident that the price they can fetch is well above what the stock is worth. After all, why should they hold an overvalued stock when there are plenty of undervalued ones out there just waiting to be purchased?

It's All About Control

Through Berkshire, when Buffett buys a business, he often buys the whole business. Yet even when he just buys some shares in a publicly traded company, he usually buys so many shares that Berkshire ends up becoming one of the largest stockholders on record. When Berkshire makes an investment, it immediately gets noticed.

When Berkshire buys the entire business, it has complete control. Buffett likes to say he does not tell good managers what to do. In fact, one reason he prefers to buy well-managed companies is that he does not want to get involved in day-to-day operations. He would much prefer to sit back and let those who understand the business best run the show. Yet there is one big difference between Buffett and almost everybody else. The fact is that because Buffett's ownership position is usually so large, he can get extremely involved in management decisions if he chooses to do so. If Buffett does not like the way the company is being run, he usually has the option to intervene and make necessary changes. If he concludes the business plan is not working, he can revamp it. If he loses faith in the managers, he can fire them and install a new team. There is absolutely no way that the average investor can do any of this. Buffett may not do it often, but he has taken a proactive approach on a number of occasions when he felt it was necessary.

For example, as we will see in chapter 6, he implemented change when dealing with problems at General Re. We will also learn that he even assumed the position of CEO at Salomon Inc. in order to save that company. Berkshire's large stake in publicly traded companies has also allowed Buffett to sit on numerous boards. In fact, he has served as a director at twenty different companies. The bottom line is that when Berkshire buys an entire company, or even when it just buys some stock in a publicly traded company, it finds itself in a position of influence. This allows Buffett to decide how that company's capital will be allocated.

How many other investors can do what Buffett does? Can you? When you make an investment, are you really thinking like Warren Buffett? Are you really thinking about controlling capital allocation decisions? Will your investment give you the option to step in and make the kinds of changes you deem necessary? If the answer to these questions is yes, then you are truly fortunate. You have the means to be a business buyer. But if the answer is no, you should realize that when you invest you are merely buying stock.

The fact is that most investors cannot do what Berkshire and Buffett do routinely. Most investors cannot buy entire companies. Indeed, they cannot even afford to buy a significant stake in any one publicly traded company. It takes $10 million to buy a 1 percent stake in a company with a billion-dollar market capitalization. And these days, a billion-dollar company is considered small. Even those who have this kind of money are not likely to commit it all to one stock. As a result, most investors will never be in a position to make the kinds of capital allocation decisions that maximize a company's returns. Whether they are willing to admit it or not, the truth is that most investors do not buy businesses. They simply cannot afford to do so.

Most investors buy stocks. And even if they were able to buy several million dollars' worth, chances are it wouldn't be enough to put them in a position to show up at company headquarters and suggest a change in business strategy. Their investment will not be sufficient to secure a seat on the board of directors. It wouldn't be enough to allow them to replace the guy who runs the mailroom let alone the CEO. At best, most investors can only hope to be free riders. This means they can buy some stock and hope that someone like Buffett steps in and purchases a large enough stake to keep management honest. Alternatively, they can simply hire Buffett to work for them directly by purchasing shares of Berkshire Hathaway.

So when you buy some stock, it may be nice to think of yourself as someone who invests like Warren Buffett. You can fantasize that you are really buying a business just as Buffett does. But if you are really honest with yourself, you will admit that you are merely buying stock. Buffett may argue that taking significant positions in a small number of companies helps control risk, but this strategy is not likely to work for the average investor. Even if they are extremely astute and know exactly what they are doing, chances are most investors will never have enough resources to take a significant position in even one company. Most investors will be able to control risk only through proper diversification. Buffett realizes this. This is why he recommends extensive diversification for most investors.

Buffett may correctly believe he is marrying the businesses he buys, but marrying stocks is simply not an appropriate strategy for everyone. The vast majority of investors do not have the resources available to marry stocks. They can only afford to date their investments. Buffett may brag that he has no exit strategy, but the average investor cannot afford to lock himself or herself into a stock forever—especially one that is providing only meager returns.

None of this is to say that ordinary investors should not invest for the long term. We have already seen that a long-term value-oriented approach works quite well. It can certainly work for you just as it has for Buffett. However, as *Forbes* columnist Ken Fisher pointed out, only Buffett can be Buffett. "Don't try to be Phil Fisher. Or Warren Buffett or Peter Lynch or anyone else. Be yourself. . . ."[2] Fisher should know what he is talking about. His father, Phil Fisher, was one of Buffett's most influential mentors. You are not Buffett and you should not assume you can invest like Buffett. As Ken Fisher says, learn to be yourself. This means you must understand who you are as an investor. What are your goals? What are your constraints? How much risk are you willing and able to tolerate? Understand which investment strategies will work best for you. Make sure you know why you are investing and how you want to invest before committing a significant portion of your wealth to any one stock, industry, or asset class.

PIPE Dreams

Here is one other thing most investors cannot do. They cannot make private investments in public equity (PIPE). This is a fascinating investment strategy often used by hedge funds. In fact, Friedland Global Capital Markets estimates that "hundreds, if not thousands of private equity funds or hedge funds have been established over the past few years to invest in PIPEs."[3] Berkshire Hathaway has also been an active PIPE investor.

As the name implies, PIPEs allow large investors to purchase equity or equity-linked securities from a public corporation through a private transaction. This arrangement saves the issuer time and money. Because it is considered a private transaction, the securities do not have to be registered with the SEC ahead of time. Furthermore, the fees involved are usually less than what the issuer would otherwise have to pay in a typical secondary offering. PIPEs also allow issuers to raise a smaller amount of money than a secondary offering typically requires. As a result, PIPEs are frequently used when the issuing company needs quick access to some meaningful amount of capital. The purchaser often gets a nice discount and the issuer promises to quickly register the securities with the SEC, thus making them liquid. It usually takes six months or less for the registration to be approved, allowing the purchaser to resell the securities to the public.

A PIPE might involve the issuance of common stock at a discount to the market price. Or, it might involve the issuance of convertible debt or convertible preferred stock. In the case of convertibles, the purchaser gets a nice yield and obtains the right to convert the security into common stock. The conversion price is usually set at a favorable level. The conversion price might be fixed, or it might be adjustable. For example, if the issuer's stock price falls, the conversion price might be reduced, allowing the issuer to garner more shares upon conversion. This arrangement provides the purchaser with an added layer of protection, but it also gives the purchaser the perverse incentive to drive down the market price of the stock by shorting it. In a PIPE transaction, the purchaser might also receive warrants that allow for the purchase of additional shares of common stock at some set exercise price.

PIPEs are often great deals for purchasers, but they are not necessarily good for the issuing company's existing shareholders. This is because they can result in a significant amount of dilution. As a result, when the market learns about a pending PIPE offering, the issuing company's stock price frequently falls in reaction. Indeed, the SEC has fined a number of hedge funds for improperly profiting from shorting shares in companies that were about to announce a PIPE issuance.[4]

Berkshire Hathaway has been involved as an investor in a number of PIPE deals. Perhaps Salomon Inc. is the best-known case. We will learn more about Berkshire's investment in Salomon in chapter 6. However, as James Altucher documents, Salomon was not Berkshire's only PIPE deal. Others include razor-blade maker Gillette, timber company Champion International, the telecom company Level 3 Communications (founded by Berkshire Hathaway director Walter Scott), and natural gas producer Williams Companies.[5] Some of these companies were healthy when Berkshire made its initial investments. Others were troubled. Yet one thing they seem to have in common is a propensity to get acquired. Salomon was eventually bought out by Travelers (now Citigroup). Gillette has since been taken over by Procter & Gamble. Champion was purchased by International Paper. So far, at least, Level 3 and Williams have managed to remain independent.

PIPEs have proven extremely profitable for many large institutional investors and Berkshire is no exception. However, for the typical individual investor, PIPEs remain nothing more than a pipe dream. Individuals who would like to participate in this market can hope to do so only indirectly by investing in a hedge fund or purchasing shares of a company like Berkshire Hathaway, which has a proven record of profiting from PIPEs.

Know Buffett Well, but Be Realistic

Warren Buffett is well known for investing in businesses rather than buying stocks. He believes all investors should do the same. He primarily opposes the short-term thinking that buying stocks implies. To a large extent he is right to think this way. There is plenty of research showing that investors who think too much about the short term often end up doing themselves harm. For example, by trading too much they might generate more profits for the brokerage firms than they do for themselves. By constantly realizing capital gains, they might produce mediocre after-tax returns even if they manage to generate excellent returns on a before-tax basis.

Marrying businesses, however, is not an appropriate strategy for ordinary investors. Instead, diversification is their best bet. Like Buffett, all investors should be smart enough to buy under-valued stocks. Unlike Buffett, however, they should be willing to sell when stocks become obviously overvalued. They should also realize that nontypical investment vehicles such as PIPEs are beyond their reach. Investors would be well advised to learn as much as they can about Buffett's favored strategies, but they should also be realistic enough to appreciate what will and what will not work for them.

KEY TAKEAWAYS: CHAPTER 4

- Buffett draws a strong distinction between buying businesses and buying stocks. He believes true investing is all about buying businesses. Those who think like business buyers make a significant financial investment and commit themselves for the long term. Those who think like stock buyers do not feel committed to their positions. They are happy to sell at the right price. Buffett eschews the idea of buying stocks rather than businesses. *Unless you have access to Buffett-like resources, it is better to think of yourself as a stock buyer than a business buyer.*

- Buffett is reluctant to sell a business under almost any circumstance. This means he will not sell a company even if it becomes seriously overvalued; and he won't sell a poor-performing business as long as it is generating some cash. He insists on sticking to this strategy even though he knows it hurts Berkshire's financial performance. *Although Buffett hates to sell under almost any circumstance, you should be willing to sell a stock when its market price far exceeds its intrinsic value. Likewise, do not feel obligated to hold on to a stock that is consistently generating a poor return on capital.*

- When Buffett buys a company on Berkshire's behalf, he buys the whole company. When he takes a position in a publicly traded stock, Berkshire usually ends up becoming one of the largest stockholders. This concentrated strategy gives Buffett a degree of influence and control ordinary investors can never hope to match. *If you don't have Buffett's business acumen or access to Buffett-like resources, diversification is your best bet for controlling risk.*

- Buffett prefers to invest in good companies with strong managers. He does not like to get involved in the management of any company, but he will not hesitate to do so when it is necessary to protect his shareholders. *The typical investor will never be in a position to influence managerial decisions.*

- Making a private investment in public equity (PIPE) is another strategy Buffett commonly employs that ordinary investors cannot utilize. By employing PIPEs, Berkshire often gets a security with a good yield that is convertible into common stock at a favorable price. *If you like the idea of employing PIPEs, invest in a company like Berkshire Hathaway or a hedge fund that has expertise and access to the PIPE market.*

5

What Buffett Buys

The larger the company, the greater will be our interest: We would like to make an acquisition in the $5–20 billion range.

—Warren Buffett[1]

As we have already seen, Berkshire Hathaway is an acquisitive company. Indeed, Berkshire is really a holding company. It owns more than seventy subsidiary companies and dozens of publicly traded stocks. Some of its subsidiary companies are quite large, such as GEICO and General Re. Others, such as Fruit of the Loom and Jordan's Furniture, are much smaller.

Although Buffett is keen to acquire companies, he does not spend an inordinate amount of time hunting for them. On the contrary, he prefers to sit back and wait for interesting deals to come to him. In fact, he openly invites business principals to contact him if they would like to consider selling their company to Berkshire. He is particularly interested in acquiring large companies involved in simple businesses with consistent earnings, little debt, and good management. But do not bother writing to Buffett about your company unless you are ready to name a price. "We don't want to waste our time or that of the seller by talking, even preliminarily, about a transaction when price is unknown."[2]

In addition, Buffett often talks about Berkshire's acquisitions in rather simplistic terms. He gives the impression that he makes quick decisions about whether or not to buy a company without having to do a tremendous amount of research or put much thought into the matter. In fact, his rather cavalier comments sometimes invite criticism of his methods. Critics have complained that Buffett makes too many "gut" decisions. Some say he does not do a sufficient amount of due diligence. The evidence, however, suggests that Buffett is very careful about what he buys. Most of the companies he purchased over the years for Berkshire have turned out to be gems. Furthermore, Buffett does not jump at every opportunity. For example, in 2004, Berkshire made no significant acquisitions at all. Buffett said, "My hope was to make several multi-billion dollar acquisitions that would add new and significant streams of earnings to the many we already have. But I struck out."[3]

One thing Buffett pays close attention to is people. He puts a tremendous amount of weight on the quality of management. His frequent remarks about the importance of good managers even give the impression that little else matters. Indeed, almost every acquisition seems to be the story of an individual—usually the founder of the company or the current CEO. After reading his comments, you might go away thinking that Buffett is convinced that as long as management is trustworthy, everything else will fall neatly into place. While it is true that Buffett prizes good managers, it is not true that he ignores everything else. There can be little doubt that Buffett also pays attention to the financials. He is not going to allow Berkshire to buy a company in some dead-end business just because he thinks the managers are wonderful people. He may enjoy giving the impression that he makes quick decisions from the gut, but you can bet that there are at least a few people at Berkshire crunching a lot of numbers behind the scenes before any deal gets the final green light.

Forest River

Berkshire bought Forest River, which controlled 19 percent of the towable recreational vehicle market, in August 2005. Ironically, Hurricane Katrina, which cost Berkshire's insurance companies a pretty penny, turned out to have a silver lining for Forest River. The company benefited from contracts to build thousands of trailers for the Federal Emergency Management Agency (FEMA). These trailers were used to house people made homeless by that horrific storm. However, the FEMA sales also came with a cloud. Not too long after buying all those trailers, FEMA started selling many of them on the secondary market. As a result, Forest River and other trailer manufacturers found themselves in direct competition with FEMA.

After reading Buffett's description of how he came to close the Forest River deal, it is easy to understand why critics sometimes accuse him of shooting from the hip. "On June 21, I received a two-page fax telling me—point by point—why Forest River met the acquisition criteria we set forth on page 25 of this report. I had not before heard of the company, a recreational vehicle manufacturer with $1.6 billion of sales, nor of Pete Liegl, its owner and manager. But the fax made sense, and I immediately asked for more figures. These came the next morning, and that afternoon I made Pete an offer."[4]

Is it really possible that Buffett decided to buy Forest River, a company he previously knew nothing about, in just twenty-four hours' time? These sound more like the actions of an impulsive day trader than those of a prudent long-term value investor like

Buffett. The Buffett we read about in books and magazines would study the situation very carefully before jumping in with both feet. Forest River might indeed be a wonderful company, but it is difficult to imagine the greatest investor of all time making what appears to be an incredibly rash decision. Where was the due diligence? What was the rush? Was Buffett worried that someone else might try to acquire Forest River at the same time? Buffett does not address these questions. He merely calls Liegl a "remarkable entrepreneur" and attaches an article to Berkshire's annual report about Forest River from a publication called *RV Business*.[5]

Although the purchase price was not disclosed, *RV Business* said speculation put it at more than $800 million, or just over one half of sales. In comparison, Thor Industries, a publicly traded recreational vehicle manufacturer, was recently selling for about 0.7 times sales. Winnebago was selling for about 1.2 times sales. It is not surprising that Berkshire purchased Forest River for what looks like a good price. Liegl, who was the sole owner of Forest River before its acquisition, stayed on to run the company on a day-to-day basis. Indeed, this is one thing almost all Berkshire acquisitions have in common. Buffett is particularly interested in buying good companies with good managers who are willing to stay put and run the show once the deal has been inked.

Business Wire

Lorry Lokey started Business Wire in 1961 with only seven clients. It took him just four months to turn a profit. The company, which distributes news for client companies and organizations, has experienced steady growth ever since. Less than ten years after Business Wire was founded, Lokey had 15 full-time employees serving more than 300 client companies. By 1990, 150 employees in 16 offices were generating $14 million a year in revenues. Ten years after that, Business Wire had 26 offices, 400 employees, and annual revenues of $40 million. By 2005, the employee count had reached 500 and annual revenues topped $125 million.

Business Wire now counts about 25,000 companies and organizations as clients. It disseminates all kinds of news and information to just about every corner of the world. Perhaps most important, it helps publicly traded companies announce quarterly financial results. Business Wire transmits these news releases to investors, journalists, regulators, and the general public. In fact, the SEC and other regulatory agencies stipulate how corporations must disseminate material nonpublic information such as earnings reports. Business Wire's services help companies satisfy these regulatory requirements. Improperly releasing information of this kind can get a company in big trouble. Nonetheless, slipups do occur. For example, Business Wire accidentally released part of Washington Mutual's earnings report before the market closed on April 18, 2006. This caused the New York Stock Exchange to halt trading in Washington Mutual stock.

After forty-five years as an independent company, Business Wire was finally acquired by Berkshire Hathaway in 2006. As Buffett explains it, newly appointed CEO Cathy Baron Tamraz read about Berkshire's acquisition of Forest River in *The Wall Street Journal* and thought that Buffett might be interested in Business Wire as well. Buffett says, "By the time I finished Cathy's two-page letter, I felt Business Wire and Berkshire were a fit."[6]

Again, this description is not consistent with the Buffett investors *think* they know. Yet it is classic Buffett in the sense that he makes it all sound so simple. He seems to be telling us that buying Business Wire was a no-brainer. It was an obvious decision that came straight from his gut. All that was left to do was shake hands and sign a few papers. Of course, it cannot possibly be this simple.

As CEO of Berkshire, Buffett is a fiduciary. He makes important decisions on behalf of his shareholders that involve hundreds of millions of dollars—sometimes more. He has an obligation to do what is best for them. Is it really possible that Buffett would allow Berkshire to buy a company purely on instinct—even if it is his own instinct? Not likely. There has got to be some serious research going on. Buffett has to make sure that proper due diligence is done. Of course, all the research in the world will not eliminate risk. But Buffett cannot afford to shoot from the hip. It may be true, as he claims, that Business Wire and Berkshire felt like a good fit, but there has got to be more to the story. You can bet a lot more went into the decision to buy Business Wire than Buffett lets on.

Buffett and Tamraz celebrated Berkshire's acquisition of Business Wire on March 20 by ringing the bell to start trading on the New York Stock Exchange. Lokey celebrated by donating $12.5 million to the University of Oregon. Despite all the festivities that were going on, it has to be pointed out that there is at least a little bit of irony in Buffett's decision to buy Business Wire. After all, Buffett has spoken critically of the stock price reaction that often takes place when a public corporation announces quarterly financial results. Yet Berkshire is now the proud owner of a company that profits from helping other companies disseminate the kind of information that serves as a catalyst for all that volatility.

Iscar Metalworking Companies

Until 2006, Buffett kept Berkshire invested solely in U.S. companies. But on July 5 of that year, Berkshire bought a foreign company for the first time in its history. You might have expected that a man like Buffett who disdains risk would have consummated Berkshire's first foreign acquisition in a major developed nation in Western Europe or East Asia. You might also have expected that he would have done a greater-than-usual amount of due diligence before agreeing to proceed with the deal. You would have been wrong on both counts.

Buffett went straight to the heart of the Middle East. Berkshire paid $4 billion to buy 80 percent of Iscar, a maker of carbide cutting tools headquartered in Tefen, Israel. Iscar has more than 6,500 employees and operates in sixty-one countries. Although Iscar's financials are not public, one estimate put annual revenues at about $1.4 billion and profits at $440 million.[7] If these figures are correct, Berkshire's purchase price values Iscar at about 3.6 times sales and 11 times earnings—not terribly expensive, but not dirt cheap either.

In case you were wondering, Tefen is in the northern part of Israel, not far from the Lebanese border. Just one week after Berkshire closed the deal, Hezbollah agents crossed into Israel from Lebanon, kidnapping two Israeli soldiers and killing several others. Israel retaliated by bombing parts of Lebanon. Hezbollah responded by indiscriminately shelling large regions of northern Israel, including Tefen.

Many American businesspeople would have thought it crazy to invest in almost any country in the Middle East. While they are all aware that no geographic region is immune to terrorism or the kind of violence that can disrupt economies, most would have preferred to look at opportunities in safer locations. Buffett, however, is a contrarian. But why did he choose Israel for Berkshire's first foreign adventure, and what was there in particular about Iscar that attracted him to that company?

By now it should come as no surprise that, like many of Berkshire's acquisitions, the Iscar deal started off with a short letter. Buffett says that just nine months before closing the deal, "I received a 1¼ page letter from Eitan [Wertheimer], of whom I then knew nothing."[8] Buffett goes on to explain that Iscar chairman Wertheimer's letter introduced Iscar and described its multinational business. One month after receiving that letter, Buffett hosted Iscar's top brass in Omaha. "A few hours with them convinced me that if we were to make a deal, we would be teaming up with extraordinarily talented managers who could be trusted to run the business after a sale with all the energy and dedication that they had exhibited previously."[9]

Berkshire has purchased a number of outstanding companies throughout the years. These include GEICO, National Indemnity, and See's Candies. Yet after visiting Iscar with his partner Charlie Munger and five other Berkshire associates two months *after* the deal closed, Buffett said, "We—and I mean every one of us—have never been more impressed with any operation."[10] Praise from Buffett does not get any stronger than this.

PacifiCorp

What have we learned so far about selling businesses to Buffett? For one thing, if you are serious about selling your company to him, make sure you keep your initial letter to less than two pages. Buffett loves simplicity, and it helps to have a business that is easy to understand. It also helps to have an outstanding management team that intends to stay in place and run the company once the deal is closed.

PacifiCorp, another Berkshire acquisition, was not the result of a two-page letter. This deal was a bit more complicated. In fact,

PacifiCorp was not a direct purchase. Instead, the company was bought by one of Berkshire's units.

PacifiCorp is a regulated public utility company that provides electricity to about 1.7 million retail customers in Utah, Oregon, Wyoming, Washington, Idaho, and California. It operates under the Rocky Mountain name in Utah, Wyoming, and Idaho. It uses the Pacific Power name in Oregon, Washington, and California. The company generates almost 80 percent of the electricity it sells, relying primarily on its eleven coal-burning plants. The remaining 20 percent of the electricity it delivers to customers is purchased on the wholesale market from other suppliers using short- and long-term contracts.

Berkshire's MidAmerican Energy unit purchased PacifiCorp in March 2006 for $5.1 billion, or 1.25 times book value. MidAmerican bought the company from ScottishPower, financing the deal with $1.7 billion of its own cash. It raised the remaining $3.4 billion by selling additional shares of common stock to Berkshire. As a result of the transaction, Berkshire increased its ownership in MidAmerican from about 81 percent to 87 percent. About 11 percent of MidAmerican is owned by Walter Scott, who is listed as an independent member of Berkshire's board of directors. Scott actually controlled 86 percent of the voting stock before Berkshire converted its preferred shares into common shares in February 2006, just one month prior to the PacifiCorp acquisition. In fact, this unusually tight-knit business relationship between Berkshire and Scott makes some Buffett watchers uneasy about his attitude toward corporate governance, which we will examine more closely in chapter 7.

PacifiCorp is a big and profitable operation—just the kind of company Buffett loves to own. For the fiscal year that ended March 2006, just before it was acquired, PacifiCorp reported earnings of $358.6 million on revenues of $3.9 billion. Return on equity was 9.7 percent. It is already making a big contribution to MidAmerican and Berkshire Hathaway. According to Berkshire's annual report, PacifiCorp accounted for 28 percent of MidAmerican's total revenues in 2006 and 21 percent of its earnings (before interest and taxes). Buffett has made it clear that he would like to consummate more purchases of companies this size or larger in the near future.

Russell Corp.

Russell Corp. was founded in 1902 and has since become a widely recognized name in the sporting goods industry. The company is well known for its athletic uniforms, sweatshirts, and T-shirts. Many professional and weekend athletes, however, do not realize that Russell also owns a number of other popular brands, including Spalding, a maker of basketballs, footballs, and baseball gloves; Moving Comfort, a maker of sports bras and other athletic wear for women; and Brooks, which specializes in running shoes and running apparel.

The apparel business has been particularly difficult in recent years as intense competition has kept selling prices and profit margins low. Russell responded by initiating a rather successful cost-cutting program in 2003. That was the same year it bought Spalding and the Bike Athletic Company, perhaps best known for its athletic supporters, or jockstraps. Thanks to acquisitions, sales in 2005 climbed 10 percent from the prior year to $1.4 billion. Unfortunately, there was no internal growth. Excluding acquisitions, sales were actually down 2 percent. Profits also fell 28 percent from 2004 to $34.4 million in 2005.

Like PacifiCorp, Russell was an indirect purchase. It was purchased by Berkshire's Fruit of the Loom unit in August 2006 for $600 million.[11] At less than one-half sales, the price looks very reasonable. But it wasn't as cheap as it might seem. Russell was a highly leveraged company when it was acquired by Fruit of the Loom. In addition to the purchase price, Berkshire ended up assuming about $600 million of additional debt. Buffett, however, loves simple companies with well-known brand names. Russell fits the bill in this respect.

Publicly Traded Stocks

In addition to buying a number of subsidiary companies, many of which we just described, Berkshire has also been accelerating the pace of common stock purchases. It still has sizable positions in the Big Four (American Express, Coca-Cola, Procter & Gamble, and Wells Fargo) and other long-term holdings (M&T Bank Corp., SunTrusts Bank, The Washington Post, and Wesco Financial Corp.). Although Berkshire listed just eight publicly traded stocks in its March 31, 1999, 13F filing, more recent filings list more than three dozen stocks.

Berkshire has taken significant positions in a number of well-known large-cap companies in recent periods. In early 2005, it purchased about 40 million shares of Anheuser-Busch for about $2 billion. The company, which makes several well-known beers including Michelob and Bud Light, produced about $2 billion in profits in 2006. Although Berkshire has since pared back its holdings a little, it still holds more than 36 million shares of the stock.

Berkshire owns about 18 million shares of ConocoPhillips, one of the world's largest integrated energy companies specializing in the exploration and production of crude oil and natural gas.

The company generates $190 billion a year in revenues. Net income in 2006 was $15.5 billion. Berkshire started buying Conoco-Phillips during the fourth quarter of 2005. Because the stock had run up 140 percent from the start of 2003 through the end of 2005, Berkshire's timing may have been a little off.

Johnson & Johnson is one of the largest companies in the health-care field. It makes consumer products, prescription medications, and medical devices. Johnson & Johnson and Boston Scientific were engaged in a bitter fight in late 2005 and early 2006 when both companies were bidding for Guidant, another medical device manufacturer. Boston Scientific won that battle, but it may have lost the war. Investors seem to have concluded it paid too much for Guidant. Berkshire made its initial investment in Johnson & Johnson by purchasing about 2 million shares during the first quarter of 2006. According to a recent SEC filing, Berkshire now owns close to 25 million shares worth about $1.5 billion.

Berkshire began buying Dun & Bradstreet in September 1999. Its initial purchase was relatively small; only about 355,000 shares worth about $10 million at the time. Dun & Bradstreet subsequently spun off Moody's Corp., which specializes in rating the credit of corporate and municipal borrowers. Moody's competes directly with Standard & Poor's. During the fourth quarter of 2000, Berkshire disclosed owning 24 million shares of Moody's common stock worth $615 million. It also owned 12 million shares of Dun & Bradstreet worth $310 million. Berkshire no longer has a position in Dun & Bradstreet, but after a two-for-one stock split in 2005, its 48 million shares of Moody's were recently worth about $3 billion.

Other well-known, large-cap companies found in the Berkshire stable at the end of 2006 included General Electric, Lowes Companies, Nike, Sanofi-Aventis, Tyco International, United

Parcel Service, Wal-Mart Stores, Burlington Northern Santa Fe, and PetroChina.[12] Most investors would not be surprised to see such names. These companies have market-leading positions in their industries. Some have market-leading positions in several industries.

A smaller company that also fits the Buffett mold is H&R Block, the leading tax-preparation service provider. Back in 1997, H&R Block entered into an agreement with Berkshire to provide its customers with information about GEICO automobile insurance. In the fourth quarter of 2000, Berkshire established a position in H&R Block by purchasing 7.7 million shares worth about $319 million. The stock was an outstanding performer, splitting two-for-one twice. In recent periods, however, Berkshire pared back its position. H&R Block is facing stiff competition in its core business from tax-preparation software sellers. At last look, Berkshire owned only 4 million post-split shares worth just $86 million.

Perhaps the most surprising name in the Berkshire portfolio is Comdisco Holding Co. This position is surprising for two reasons: it involves technology *and* bankruptcy. Those are two words people do not normally associate with Warren Buffett. Berkshire owns 1.5 million shares of Comdisco Holding, which was formed in 2002 for the purpose of liquidating the remaining assets of Comdisco, Inc., a technology equipment leasing company that filed for bankruptcy in 2001. Berkshire disclosed its position in Comdisco Holding in late 2002. In early 2003, the stock was selling in the mid-80s, giving Berkshire's position a $120 million value. More recently, however, Comdisco Holding was selling for about $12 per share. Berkshire's position at the time was worth about $18 million.

Most investors would also be extremely surprised by the

turnover found in Berkshire's portfolio since 2000. Buffett, of
course, is the same man investors like to believe holds stocks forever. He is the man who says you should invest like a business
buyer, not a stock trader. Yet in recent years, a rather large number
of stocks were added, then quickly dropped from Berkshire's stable. Some of the better-known names include Citigroup, Walt
Disney, Best Buy, Gap Inc., Duke Energy, and Cadbury
Schweppes. These and many others are listed in Table 5.1.

Table 5.1

**Some of the Stocks Added to and Dropped from Berkshire
Hathaway's Portfolio Since 2000**

Liz Claiborne	Omnicom
Jones Apparel	Best Buy
Citigroup	Gap Inc.
Walt Disney	Level 3 Communications
GATX Corp.	Duke Energy
La-Z-Boy	HCA Inc.
Sealed Air	Cadbury Schweppes
Mueller Industries	Dean Foods
Dover Corp.	Lexmark International

KEY TAKEAWAYS: CHAPTER 5

- Buffett is keen to acquire companies, but he is in no hurry to buy. He prefers to wait for the right opportunity, and he does not hesitate to sit on his cash if nothing piques his interest. *Money will not burn a hole in your pocket. Do not buy a stock just because you have cash waiting to be put to work. Wait until the right opportunity comes along.*

- Because he often talks about Berkshire's acquisitions in simplistic terms, critics sometimes say he does not do a sufficient amount of due diligence. Rest assured, however, that Buffett and his staff do their homework before committing their shareholders' funds. *If you are planning to invest for the long term like Buffett, make sure you thoroughly do your homework on a company before you buy the stock. Proper due diligence today can prevent a lot of regrets tomorrow.*

- Buffett is keen on buying companies with good management. This is because he does not want to get involved in day-to-day operations. He would much rather aggregate the cash flows good companies can produce, and then make decisions on how that capital should be reinvested. *Long-term investors should pay particular attention to the quality of management. Make sure top management has a significant stake. Also, you do not want to invest in a company whose key personnel are looking to cash out or retire.*

- Iscar was Berkshire's first acquisition outside the United States. Buffett claims he "has never been more impressed with any other operation." *In the future, much of the world's economic growth will take place outside the United States. Consider buying foreign stocks (preferably through international mutual funds or ADRs on U.S. exchanges), and do not be afraid to commit some funds to companies in less stable parts of the world.*

- Although they are subject to regulation, Buffett is a big fan of utility companies. In 2006, about $900 million of Berkshire's $11 billion in net earnings came from its MidAmerican subsidiary. *A well-run utility company can generate a steady flow of cash. Utilities should be a core holding in your portfolio.*

- Although Berkshire holds on to its subsidiary companies for the long term, its portfolio of publicly traded stocks has exhibited significant turnover in recent years. Well-known stocks that have spent little time in the portfolio include Citigroup, Duke Energy, Best Buy, Gap, and PetroChina. Relatively recent purchases include Burlington Northern Santa Fe, Anheuser-Busch, ConocoPhillips, Johnson & Johnson, General Electric, Wal-Mart, and Tyco International. *If it no longer makes sense to keep a stock in your portfolio, do not hesitate to sell it. Contrary to popular opinion, even Buffett trades stocks.*

6

When "Good" Investments Go Bad

I was dead wrong.   —Warren Buffett, 2002, 2005

As we have seen, if you play it like Buffett, investing is a game that requires a great deal of patience. Rarely are the results immediate. Nor are they always obvious. Buffett's record shows that an investment that quickly sours and looks like a strikeout might actually end up becoming a home run many years down the road. On the other hand, an investment that at first looks like a sure winner could end up becoming a costly error. You certainly don't want to celebrate prematurely.

In baseball terms, Warren Buffett has had plenty of hits. Many have eventually turned out to be home runs. GEICO, National Indemnity, See's Candies, Borsheim's Fine Jewelry, Coca-Cola, Wells Fargo, American Express, The Washington Post, and Gillette (which was acquired by Procter & Gamble in 2005) are among his best investments. Yet, as difficult as it is to believe, Buffett has also made some costly errors. Of course, this only serves to prove he is human. Fortunately for Berkshire's shareholders, Buffett's errors have been few and far between. But they remind us that no investor, not even Buffett, can have a perfect record.

Buffett is an investor, not a manager. In fact, he hates getting involved in the management of the companies he acquires. This is why he insists on buying companies with good managers already in place. "At Berkshire, we don't tell .400 hitters how to swing."[1] Yet Buffett has also been known to step in and call the shots when there are obvious problems. He says he hates firing people, but like all good managers, he will do what he has to do in order to protect his shareholders. As you will see in this chapter, if need be, Buffett will even step in and personally run the business in order to save it.

Buffett is also suspicious of acquisitions that are financed with equity. He thinks if it really makes sense to buy a business, the acquirer should be willing to pay cash. Yet we will also learn in this chapter that in 1998 he financed the purchase of two companies with at least some Berkshire stock. Both turned out to be troubled investments.

And even though Buffett has a reputation for being a long-term investor, he also knows when to cut and run. He is not averse to taking his losses and getting out of a position if he becomes convinced that there isn't much hope for a turnaround.

Buffett's successes have been thoroughly analyzed in many publications already written about him; and studying his successes is certainly instructive. This chapter, however, takes a look at four of Buffett's more troubling investments. The purpose of doing this is not to embarrass the man. Indeed, given his investment record, embarrassing Buffett is nearly impossible. He has absolutely nothing to be ashamed of. Readers should understand, however, that sometimes there is as much to learn from an outstanding investor's mistakes and failures as there is from his successes. In addition, knowing that great investors also make mistakes can help you form more reasonable expectations about your own investment performance.

To reiterate, we cannot even be sure if a troubled investment will end up becoming a success or failure until many years down the road. Berkshire has made a number of investments that did not look so hot in the beginning, but eventually ended up making good money for shareholders. That is certainly the case with the first example in this chapter. The full story for the next two examples has yet to be written. Buffett, however, has already thrown in the towel on the last one.

Salomon Inc.

Salomon Inc.[2] provides the most obvious example of Buffett stepping in and taking charge. Begun as a partnership in 1910, Salomon Brothers was one of Wall Street's most prestigious investment banks. In the 1980s, it was perhaps the world's preeminent fixed-income house, credited with developing innovative products such as mortgage-backed securities. Salomon was a tremendously successful company, but some saw it as arrogant. Tom Wolfe, author of *The Bonfire of the Vanities,* is believed to have modeled his lead character, Sherman McCoy, whom he refers to as a "Master of the Universe," after the bond traders at Salomon.

Berkshire's initial investment in Salomon did not simply begin with Buffett buying some shares of common stock. Instead, as he often does, he negotiated a special deal. He agreed to purchase $700 million worth of convertible preferred stock. As we saw in chapter 4, this kind of private investment in public equity is referred to by the acronym PIPE. It has become Berkshire's modus operandi in many of its large investments. It provides an excellent example of what Buffett and Berkshire do that ordinary investors cannot do.

Salomon cut the deal with Berkshire because it needed the cash to buy back some of its own common stock from a group of share-holders who were considering selling to Ronald Perelman. Salomon's management viewed Perelman as a hostile bidder, but they considered Buffett's company, Berkshire Hathaway, a much friendlier force. Along with his investment, Buffett was given a seat on Salomon's board.

At first, things were going great. Berkshire's investment looked smart as Salomon's shares climbed. But then things soured. It turned out that Salomon had a rogue trader on its staff who tried to bypass Treasury Department rules designed to prevent any single entity from cornering the government bond market. What's worse, when management discovered the problem it failed to re-port it promptly to regulators or to its own board of directors. Quite reluctantly, Buffett stepped in as CEO in 1991 to save Salomon. Most important, he was able to convince the Treasury Department to reverse a decision it had made that would have banned Salomon from bidding at future government bond auctions. That ban would have ended Salomon's ability to conduct business. It would have forced the company into bankruptcy. It also would have destroyed the value of Berkshire's substantial investment in the company. Worse still, it could have caused havoc in financial markets around the world.

Interestingly, John Meriwether, who began arbitraging ineffi-ciencies in bond prices in 1975 while working at Salomon, was one of the players caught up in the Salomon fiasco.[3] If the name sounds familiar, it is because Meriwether played a much bigger role in another financial mess that could have created severe repercussions for world markets. Meriwether was the founder of Long-Term Capital Management, the now infamous hedge fund that collapsed in 1998 and had to be bailed out at the last minute by creditors in a meeting orchestrated by the Federal Reserve Bank of New York.

Thanks to Buffett, Salomon was saved. In 1992, he stepped down as CEO. Five years later Salomon was purchased by Travelers Group, which is now part of Citigroup. Perhaps surprisingly, Berkshire made good money on its Salomon investment. In fact, it made about 2.5 times its initial investment in about ten years. So can Salomon really be considered a troubled investment? Was it not really a success for Berkshire and its shareholders? From an investment return perspective, Salomon was indeed a success. However, it is impossible to believe that Buffett would have invested in Salomon if he had had any inkling of the kind of crisis the company was about to confront. Although Salomon turned out to be a profitable investment, it put Buffett in an unenviable position he no doubt would have preferred to avoid.

General Re

General Re is a reinsurance company, which means it is an insurance company for insurance companies. Just as you might buy insurance to protect yourself against a loss to property, the company you purchase that policy from might buy insurance to protect itself from incurring a loss in the event you make a claim.

Berkshire purchased General Re at the end of 1998 for $22 billion, an absolutely massive amount of money then, as now. General Re shareholders were compensated for their sale with a combination of cash and Berkshire stock. This in itself was unusual for Buffett. He has an aversion to paying for acquisitions with stock. In fact, in 1996 he issued to shareholders a pamphlet that listed "Owner-Related Business Principles." He often refers to this pamphlet as Berkshire's "Owner's Manual." Principle #10 discusses his reluctance to issue Berkshire common stock for any purpose. However, Buffett says Berkshire "will consider issuing stock when we receive as much in intrinsic business value as we give up."[4]

Buffett loves the insurance business. Indeed, Berkshire's tremendous success over the years is largely due to his big bet on this one industry. One reason Buffett loves this business is because of its access to "float." *Float* refers to the difference between the premiums an insurance company receives and the claims it pays out. Because claims are typically not paid until many years after the premiums start coming in, float can be substantial. Of course, the insurance company does not simply sit on the float. It puts it to work. It buys financial securities such as stocks and bonds so it can try to earn a handsome rate of return. Thanks to the General Re acquisition, Berkshire's average float jumped from just $7 billion in 1997 to almost $23 billion at the end of 1998.

Despite all that float, however, things did not get off to a good start. In his 1999 letter to shareholders Buffett said "we had a huge—and, I believe, aberrational—underwriting loss at General Re."[5] Buffett decided General Re was not charging enough for its policies. Because of competition, businesses often cut prices in order to capture market share and increase overall sales. But excessively aggressive pricing strategies can end up hurting a company's bottom line. By underpricing its policies, General Re was cutting its own profits. Buffett decided he needed to raise rates. He knew premiums earned would decline, but he said "if there is no mega-catastrophe in 2000, the company's underwriting loss should fall considerably."[6]

As shown in Table 6.1, General Re's premiums earned did in fact fall as Buffett expected—perhaps more so. In fact, premiums earned fell 30 percent for the six years ending in December 2006. Most of the decline occurred in the company's North American property/casualty business. Interestingly, there is one other item of note about General Re in Buffett's 1999 letter to shareholders: despite the disappointing financial performance, Buffett expressed confidence in Ron Ferguson, General Re's CEO. This is a statement he undoubtedly regrets making.

Table 6.1
General Re's Premiums Earned
($ millions)

2000	8,696
2001	8,353
2002	8,500
2003	8,245
2004	7,245
2005	6,435
2006	6,075

Although things did get better in 2000, Buffett expressed concern about the cost of float. Yet he seemed confident that float costs would decline. He said there was still much work to do at General Re, but he appeared satisfied that insurance policies were now being priced more appropriately. He was also pleased that

General Re's profitability was returning to past standards. And as he does almost every year, he again spoke in prophetic terms about catastrophes, saying, "If there's no mega-catastrophe in 2001, General Re's float cost should fall materially."[7]

Unfortunately, Buffett's dreaded mega-catastrophe actually occurred when terrorists attacked America on September 11, 2001. While others were left dumbfounded wondering how anyone could have possibly foreseen such a terrible tragedy, in characteristic fashion, Buffett blamed himself. "I allowed General Re to take on business without a safeguard I knew was important, and on September 11th, this error caught up with us."[8]

Buffett went on to explain the three key principles of the insurance business: (1) Accept only risks you can properly evaluate, (2) Make sure the risks you accept are not correlated with one another so that no single event threatens solvency, and (3) No matter how profitable, don't do business with bad people.

He said he had failed to properly implement the first two principles at General Re. He also said General Re had been too aggressive in going after business. By this he meant policies were still not being priced accordingly. He promised to restore underwriting discipline. Berkshire estimated its pretax underwriting loss due to the September 11 terror attacks at $2.4 billion ($1.9 billion from General Re alone), reducing the company's net earnings by $1.5 billion. Ironically, just a short while before the terrorists launched their attacks, it was decided that Ron Ferguson, the man Buffett had praised just two years earlier, would soon step down as CEO. Ferguson was replaced by Joe Brandon.

Buffett also disclosed in that same letter that $800 million of costs were charged against 2001 earnings because General Re's reserves in prior years had understated liabilities. Although he assured shareholders that this was an honest mistake, he said it resulted in overstated profits and undeserved incentive compensation in earlier years.

There was one other very interesting detail in the 2001 letter. The letter disclosed a decision to "commence a long-term run-off of GRS."[9] GRS stands for General Re Securities, a unit of General Re, which was engaged in derivatives trading presumably for the purpose of hedging risk. GRS was about to become one of Buffett's biggest headaches.

In the 2002 annual report, Buffett applauded Joe Brandon for restoring underwriting discipline at General Re. Yet Buffett also seemed to express regret about making the acquisition. When he made the decision to buy General Re, Buffett thought the company was practicing proper underwriting discipline and that reserve policies were conservative. However, in his 2002 letter to shareholders he said, "I was dead wrong."[10]

Nonetheless, Buffett seemed convinced that the worst was over and that General Re was making a long-awaited turnaround. Then he unveiled another problem. He said GRS had lost $173 million in pretax profits due to derivatives trading. Although Buffett admitted, "I sometimes engage in large-scale derivatives transactions to facilitate certain investment strategies,"[11] he devoted three pages to a disquisition of the enormous dangers posed by derivatives. This is the same letter containing Buffett's famous declaration labeling derivatives "financial weapons of mass destruction."[12]

One year later Buffett proclaimed General Re's problems fixed. As shown in Table 6.2 (page 132), General Re turned in an underwriting profit for the first time since Berkshire purchased the company in December 1998. While underwriting losses are not uncommon in the insurance industry, they are certainly not the norm for Berkshire-owned insurance companies. Buffett praised Joe Brandon and his partner Tad Montross for doing a great job of putting General Re back on the right track. At the same time, however, he said derivatives had hurt General Re's pretax profits to the tune of $99 million in 2003 (Table 6.3). Once again he blamed himself for not being more diligent, saying he could have saved shareholders at least $100 million if he had acted more expeditiously to unwind derivatives contracts and shut down GRS.

Table 6.2
General Re's Pretax Underwriting Gain/(Loss)
($ millions)

1999	(1,184)
2000	(1,254)
2001	(3,671)
2002	(1,393)
2003	145
2004	3
2005	(334)
2006	526

Table 6.3
General Re Securities Derivatives Losses
($ millions)

2002	173
2003	99
2004	44
2005	104
2006	5

Things continued to improve in 2004. Despite hurricane-related losses of $1.25 billion, General Re managed to turn in another underwriting profit, albeit a small one. In addition, derivatives losses at GRS declined to just $44 million. But 2004 was the calm before the storm—literally. As bad as the 2004 hurricane season was, 2005 was much worse. That was the year Katrina drowned New Orleans. All in all, Katrina and other hurricanes cost Berkshire $3.4 billion in 2005. However, the bulk of the losses was in Berkshire's other insurance units.

Thanks to Buffett's insistence that General Re institute a more conservative approach to underwriting, General Re's hurricane-related losses in 2005 amounted to only $685 million. While this was an encouraging sign that General Re was finally fixed, GRS continued to mount losses from unwinding its derivative positions, losing $104 million in 2005. The good news, however, was that 95 percent of its derivatives risks had been eliminated. Buffett was confident that future losses from this unit would be immaterial.

He was right about that. GRS derivatives losses amounted to only $5 million in 2006. Perhaps more important, at the end of that year, there were only 197 contracts left to unwind. This was down from 23,218 when the process began in 2002. In general, 2006 turned out to be a banner year for all of Berkshire's insurance units. General Re's pretax underwriting gain went strongly into the black.

General Re has certainly given Buffett many financial headaches. Unfortunately, it has given him some legal ones, too. For example, the U.S. attorney for the Eastern District of Virginia subpoenaed General Re and several of its employees in connection with an investigation of Reciprocal of America, which went into liquidation proceedings. Reciprocal was a reinsurer that specialized in medical liability risks.

Two General Re units, General Reinsurance Australia (GRA) and Kölnische Ruckversicherungs-Gesellschaft (KR), were accused of helping FAI Insurance Limited improperly account for reinsurance transactions. It is alleged that with the help of reinsurance policies FAI was able to convert losses into paper gains, which duped HIH Insurance Limited into paying too high a price in 1998 when it acquired FAI.

American International Group (AIG), formerly run by the colorful Maurice "Hank" Greenberg, admitted to using reinsurance contracts to manipulate earnings rather than for legitimate risk transfer purposes. AIG paid $1.64 billion to settle civil fraud charges. Unfortunately for Buffett, General Re wrote those reinsurance contracts. Four former General Re executives, including Ron Ferguson, were indicted on charges of participating in AIG's scheme. Although Ferguson had stepped down as CEO in 2001, he was still providing consulting services to General Re. However, his services were terminated by General Re in 2005, right after Ferguson invoked his Fifth Amendment rights rather than answer questions posed by regulators relating to the AIG case.

In November 2006, the Financial Services Authority of the United Kingdom fined General Re £1.2 million (about $2.3 million) for arranging improper reinsurance contracts. One of these contracts apparently helped a German insurance company obtain tax advantages by transferring funds to its subsidiary in Ireland.

It is important to note that many of General Re's financial and legal problems date back to before Berkshire's acquisition of the company. Under Buffett's watch, General Re has been cleaning up its act. Perhaps some day, General Re will turn out to be one of Berkshire's hits. It may even become a home run. Yet there is no question that it must be counted among Buffett's more troubled acquisitions. It is difficult to believe Buffett would have purchased General Re back in 1998 if he knew then what he knows now.

NetJets

Berkshire purchased NetJets (formerly known as Executive Jet) for $725 million in 1998. That is the same year it bought General Re. And as it did for the General Re acquisition, Berkshire paid for NetJets using a combination of cash and stock. Given Buffett's well-known aversion to using stock to pay for acquisitions, perhaps we should not be surprised to learn that, like General Re, NetJets turned out to be a troublesome purchase.

NetJets is certainly an interesting and innovative business. It sells fractional shares in airplanes. Customers who purchase these shares are entitled to a certain amount of flying time each year. In addition to buying the fractional shares, customers must pay for actual flying time as well as monthly management fees. Flying with NetJets is considerably more expensive than flying commercial, yet it is substantially less expensive than purchasing and maintaining an entire plane and crew for dedicated use.

The typical NetJets customer is a corporation or a high-net-worth individual who travels a lot and frequently needs to make flight plans on very short notice. In fact, NetJets claims it requires only four hours' notice to have a plane available and ready to go at an airport of the customer's choosing. Buffett had been a NetJets customer for several years before Berkshire bought the company. It turns out NetJets had also been a Berkshire customer.

NetJets' pilots receive their training from FlightSafety International, another one of Berkshire's subsidiary companies.

Things started off well enough, with NetJets immediately contributing to Berkshire's overall revenues and profits. However, Buffett soon warned that margins in this business were thin. In particular, expansion efforts in Europe and a strong emphasis on safety were making it difficult for NetJets to grow the bottom line. NetJets was unable to translate strong revenue growth in Europe into profits. And from the very beginning, both Buffett and NetJets CEO Rich Santulli insisted that safety was of paramount concern. They have always shown a willingness to spend whatever is necessary to ensure the safety of their passengers. For example, pilots go through rigorous training programs twice a year. They actually get more training than the Federal Aviation Administration requires. And unlike competing companies, NetJets trains each pilot to fly only one kind of airplane. Yet at the same time, NetJets offers customers a variety of planes to choose from. The company's fleet includes planes made by several different manufacturers. Other fractional ownership companies are affiliated with just one manufacturer, which facilitates pilot training and helps keep costs down.

Because NetJets and FlightSafety International are intertwined, until 2005, Berkshire lumped their results together into one segment called Flight Services. Ever since NetJets was acquired, it was the segment's bigger driver of revenue growth. As shown in Table 6.4, segment revenues increased 12 percent annually over the six years ending in 2005. Unfortunately, NetJets was also the primary reason why segment profits fell 47 percent during the same time. In 2001, NetJets even contributed to Berkshire's higher debt load when it borrowed money to "finance aircraft inventory and core fleet acquisitions."[13]

Table 6.4

Berkshire's Flight Services Segment Revenues and Operating Profits ($ millions)

YEAR	REVENUES	OPERATING PROFITS
1998	858	181
1999	1,856	225
2000	2,279	213
2001	2,563	186
2002	2,837	225
2003	2,431	72
2004	3,244	191
2005	3,660	120

Segment operating profits took a nice jump in 2002. But the increase was not the result of improving operations. Instead, it came from a $60 million onetime gain from the sale of a Boeing partnership interest. Likewise the big drop in profits in 2003 was blamed on onetime write-downs of flight simulators and aircraft inventory. It turns out that even FlightSafety was experiencing the effects of an industry slowdown. Yet FlightSafety was a gem compared to NetJets. Even though NetJets was making money in the United States, it posted a $41 million pretax loss in 2003 because of continued problems in Europe. This marked at least the third year in a row that NetJets lost money.

Things improved somewhat in 2004, with NetJets making a $10 million pretax profit. Consistent with trends, however, the company continued to lose money in Europe. Nonetheless, Buffett stressed again the importance of the European market to the company's future success. Although he admitted that operating in Europe was "far more expensive than I anticipated,"[14] he remained optimistic that momentum was building and that the red ink would soon turn black.

In 2005 Buffett said, "I was dead wrong." These are the same words he used in 2002 when describing underwriting discipline and reserve policies at General Re. They are not words Berkshire shareholders like to hear. FlightSafety was doing well, having recovered from the industry slowdown. NetJets, however, was still struggling. Buffett had been right about things getting better in Europe. Unfortunately, he was caught by surprise when profits in the United States turned to losses. Because of shortages of aircraft, NetJets was forced to rely on expensive charter services to meet its contractual obligations. As a result, the company lost $80 million in 2005.

During the Internet boom of the late 1990s, analysts often joked about online retailers with booming sales but no profits. The joke was that they were selling goods that cost them a dollar for only ninety cents, but they were hoping to make up the difference on volume. NetJets seemed to be in a similar situation. Revenues were growing rather impressively. Unfortunately, so were the losses.

In Berkshire's 2006 annual report Buffett called the situation at NetJets "*much* improved." He said demand was finally booming in Europe and that U.S. operations improved over 2005 levels. Buffett said NetJets made pretax profits of $143 million for the year, up nicely from the pretax loss of $80 million in 2005. Since the company is committed to purchasing 483 new aircraft through 2015, it is a very encouraging sign to see that NetJets may finally be out of the woods.

In all fairness to Buffett and Berkshire, NetJets, which has the largest market share, is not the only fractional aircraft business that has struggled in recent years. Flexjet, owned by aircraft manufacturer Bombardier, lost money for a decade before it finally turned a small profit in 2006. But Bombardier does not care so much about making money on its Flexjet operation. Instead, it appears to be more interested in using the business to create buzz for its airplanes. The same applies to Flight Options, which is owned by Raytheon.

Until very recently, Berkshire had not had much luck in the aviation business. In the 1990s, it had a stake in the troubled airline US Airways. The fractional aircraft business has also proven to be a difficult one. After all, when several customers own a piece of an airplane and each is entitled to use it with only a few hours' notice, problems will inevitably arise. What happens when everyone wants to fly on a Friday afternoon or a Monday morning? It is prohibitively expensive to charter airplanes on short notice to satisfy each customer's request. In addition, planes must often be flown empty. If a customer wants a plane in Albuquerque four hours from now, it has to get there somehow from someplace. If the operator has another customer who just happens to want to arrive in Albuquerque at about the same time, that's great. If not, the operator has to absorb the cost of flying the plane there empty. Properly managing these so-called deadhead flights is critical to profitability.

Truth be told, NetJets just does not seem to fit the Buffett mold. For one thing, it is an extremely capital-intensive business. Although the largest plane in the NetJets fleet holds eighteen passengers, even a small seven-seat jet costs several million dollars. On top of that, there are maintenance and operating expenses, pilot training costs, and salaries for the crew. It is difficult to see how the business can be profitable without some kind of synergistic relationship with an aircraft manufacturer or commercial airline company.

The fractional aircraft business is not like Berkshire's other businesses. It does not appear to have anything in common with insurance, candy, soft drinks, or razor blades. It seems to be a much more difficult business from which to make money. Nonetheless, if anyone can make money in this business, it is Buffett. Given his exemplary track record, there is a reasonably good chance that someday he will figure out a way to make NetJets work. Yet at this juncture, it is difficult to understand why Buffett was so keen to buy the company in the first place.

Pier 1 Imports

Pier 1 Imports is primarily a furniture retailer. In fact, furniture accounts for about 40 percent of the company's sales. But Pier 1 also sells related items such as lamps and vases, dinnerware, bath products, candles, bedding, and various seasonal items for the home.

Back in the 1990s, Pier 1 was a very hot stock. It rallied all the way from about $3.50 per share in 1994 to $20 per share in 1998. However, investors started dumping the stock in mid-1998 because of concerns that growth was slowing. The stock eventually bottomed out around $5.50 per share about a year later. Then it commenced another strong rally. This rally also lasted four years and took the stock all the way up to about $25 per share by the end of 2003. During fiscal 2003, which ended March 1, Pier 1 opened ninety new stores net. Total store count had climbed to

1,074 from 763 just five years earlier. For fiscal 2003, Pier 1 reported a 13 percent surge in sales to $1.7 billion. Net income jumped 29 percent to $129 million or $1.36 per share. At the time, Pier 1 was truly a growth stock.

Whenever a company or industry reports strong growth and outstanding financial results, it does not take long before it attracts attention—and not just from investors. High profits invite competition. In fact, that is what competition is all about. Unless there are significant barriers to entry, competitors will go after those profits until they eliminate them, or at least drive them down to more normal levels. And Pier 1 certainly faces its share of stiff competition. In addition to specialty retailers Bed Bath & Beyond, Williams-Sonoma, Restoration Hardware, Pottery Barn, and Cost Plus, it also has to fend off megadiscounters such as Wal-Mart, Target, and Costco.

Revenue growth soon slowed. In fiscal 2004 revenues advanced just 6 percent to $1.8 billion. Same-store sales actually fell 2.6 percent. Net income fell 9 percent to $118 million, yet the company still earned a respectable $1.29 per share. Unfortunately, things continued to deteriorate. Total sales were flat in fiscal 2005, but same-store sales dropped more than 6 percent. Net income plunged 49 percent to $60.5 million. Earnings dropped to 71 cents per share.

Despite these problems, there was something about Pier 1 that caught Buffett's eye. Berkshire Hathaway purchased 8 million shares during the second quarter of 2004. It is not exactly clear how much Berkshire paid for the stock, but during that quarter, Pier 1's stock price ranged from a low of $17 to a high of $23. Assuming Berkshire paid an average price of $19 per share, it would have invested about $150 million into Pier 1 common stock.

It also is not clear why Buffett was interested in Pier 1. Perhaps he thought it would fit strategically with certain Berkshire subsidiaries such as Jordan's Furniture and Nebraska Furniture Mart. Furniture sales often do well when the housing market is strong, and we know Buffett was bullish on housing at the time because he had recently purchased Clayton Homes. Maybe Buffett just thought Pier 1 stock was way oversold. If he was convinced that Pier 1's recent earnings shortfalls were just an aberration, it would make sense to start accumulating the shares.

The market found out about Berkshire's 8 million share purchase of Pier 1 on August 17, 2004, through Berkshire's 13F filing with the SEC. Pier 1 closed 8.7 percent higher that day (see Figure 6.1). This kind of reaction is often termed the "Buffett Effect." When others find out what Buffett is buying, they often jump in and bid the stock price higher. In this particular case they were probably betting that if someone as smart as Buffett was buying Pier 1, everyone else must have been missing something. Perhaps Pier 1 really was an oversold stock.

Unfortunately, the "Buffett" rally was short lived. Pier 1's operations continued to deteriorate. Total sales fell 2.7 percent in fiscal 2006. Same-store sales plunged another 7 percent. The bottom line turned red as the company lost $39.8 million, or 32 cents per share. The stock fell down to $10.50 per share. Buffett fans like to believe Buffett rarely sells. They have heard that his favorite holding period is forever. They know that when a stock's price falls, Buffett often takes the opportunity to buy more shares and reduce his average purchase price.

Not this time. Buffett apparently decided that buying more shares of Pier 1 would simply be throwing good money after bad. Instead, during the third quarter of 2005, just about a year after he began buying Pier 1, he reduced Berkshire's investment in the

Figure 6.1

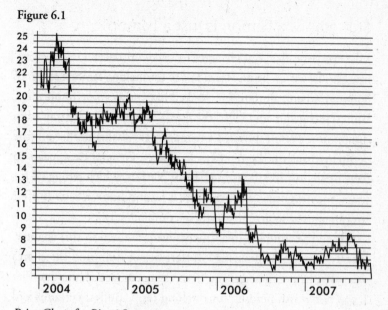

Price Chart for Pier 1 Imports *(Source: Telemet America)*

stock. That quarter he unloaded 4.71 million shares. Pier 1 ranged in price between $11 and $14.50 per share during the quarter. This means Berkshire likely lost at least $20 million on the shares it sold. Although $20 million is chump change for Berkshire, Buffett could not have been pleased. Berkshire continued to pare down its Pier 1 holdings and no longer owns any of the stock. At last look, Pier 1 was selling in the single digits. As stated earlier, it is not clear why Buffett started buying Pier 1 in the first place. It is also not clear what eventually convinced him to give up and sell. What is clear, however, is that Pier 1 was one of Buffett's rare mistakes. It turned out to be a money-losing investment for Berkshire and its shareholders.

Sometimes a Lemon Is Just a Lemon

Like everyone else, Buffett hates to make mistakes. Unlike everyone else, however, he has a real knack for making lemonade out of lemons. When Salomon Inc. looked like it was going to blow up, Buffett stepped in and saved the day. When General Re started to disappoint, Buffett initiated a management shakeout that put the company back on the right track. Today, General Re appears to have finally turned the corner. Even NetJets, which struggled for years, may eventually prove to be a resounding success. Buffett simply refused to give up on these companies.

Of all the troubled investments we examined in this chapter, Pier 1 is the most puzzling. Buffett began dumping the shares soon after he purchased them. Something convinced him that Pier 1 was not worth holding for the long term. Buffett certainly did not take long to throw in the towel on this investment. While he and his Berkshire shareholders lost money on Pier 1, at least he was quick to realize his mistake and get out of the investment as rapidly as he reasonably could.

KEY TAKEAWAYS: CHAPTER 6

- Buffett has made many outstanding investments over the years on Berkshire's behalf, but his record is not perfect. However, it can take years to find out if a particular investment was a smart move or just an unfortunate mistake. *If you are investing for the long term, do not break out the champagne just because a recent investment immediately rallies. Likewise, do not be discouraged if it quickly sours. If the business is sound, there is a good chance it will eventually recover and prove profitable.*

- Buffett prefers not to get involved in the management of companies, but he will do what he has to in order to protect his shareholders. The most obvious example of this was when he assumed the role of CEO at Salomon Inc. in 1991. Buffett's involvement saved Salomon, and Berkshire earned a nice profit when Salomon was eventually sold to Travelers Group. *If you own stock in a troubled company, your investment is more likely to pay off if there are one or more activist investors willing to take on management and shake things up.*

- Buffett prefers not to finance acquisitions with stock, but he allowed Berkshire to pay $22 billion for General Re in 1998 using a combination of cash and stock. At first, the purchase looked like a no-brainer, more than tripling Berkshire's float. But General Re kept incurring large underwriting losses. Buffett soon discovered accounting irregularities and problems with derivatives contracts. General Re was even implicated in a number of legal issues, including AIG's use of reinsurance contracts to manipulate earnings. Even though General Re's troubles finally seem to be over, Buffett no doubt would have preferred that things had gone more smoothly. *Acquisitions can be extremely risky. Acquirers should always remember the Latin phrase* caveat emptor. *Be wary if you own shares in a company that makes a habit of financing acquisitions with stock rather than cash.*

- Also in 1998, Berkshire purchased NetJets for a combination of cash and stock. Revenue growth was impressive from the very start, but NetJets kept incurring losses for many years. Buffett and CEO Rich Santulli were determined to expand operations in Europe, but costs were much higher than expected. It took eight years before the company was able to turn in a decent profit. *Capital-intensive businesses are best avoided unless the company has obvious advantages over competitors, such as barriers to entry that cannot be breached or synergies with partners that cannot be easily duplicated.*

- Pier 1 Imports is a publicly traded furniture retailer. It experienced tremendous growth prior to 2004. Berkshire began buying the common stock after Pier 1 reported disappointing financial results and the stock came off its highs. Unfortunately, operations continued to deteriorate. Just over a year after buying Pier 1, Berkshire began unloading the stock. *Just because the stock of a high-growth company plunges, that does not necessarily make it a "buy."*

7

Governance and the Next Buffett

*The least independent directors are likely to be those who
receive an important fraction of their income from the fees they
receive for board service (and who hope as well to be recommended for election to other boards and thereby to boost their
income further). Yet these are the very board members most
often classified as "independent."*

—Warren Buffett, 2004

Investors are generally convinced that Warren Buffett is a shareholder rights activist. After all, he has been extremely critical of
CEOs and other executives who seem more interested in enrich-
ing themselves than in doing what is best for their shareholders.
While no one could reasonably accuse Buffett of doing the same,
critics argue that Berkshire's corporate governance and succession
planning have left much to be desired, at least until very recently.

Governance and succession planning have always been critical
issues, but they jumped to the forefront after a number of corporate scandals made front-page news. Tyco International was run
by a CEO who looted the company while the directors were either
unaware of what was going on or simply looked the other way.

Enron, WorldCom, Adelphia, and a handful of other companies went bust in part because of poor corporate governance practices that gave their CEOs too much autonomy with too little oversight. Investors began screaming for more independent and responsible boards of directors. Politicians soon responded by introducing more regulation.

Governance is not a concern for a small business owned and run by a single proprietor. After all, a sole owner who is also the manager hurts only himself when he takes money from the till or makes business decisions that prove to be unwise. But things change dramatically when the company goes public and the number of owners increases. Indeed, the issue of governance arises from the separation of ownership and control in typical public corporations. If the CEO owns half the stock and embezzles a million dollars, his theft personally costs him $500,000. But if he owns just 1 percent of the stock, his million-dollar theft costs him just $10,000. The rest is paid for out of the pockets of the remaining shareholders.

Public corporations are usually run by professional managers who are hired by boards of directors who themselves are elected by shareholders. Directors and managers have a fiduciary responsibility to do what is best for shareholders. They are obligated to put the shareholders' interests ahead of their own. This typically means making decisions that maximize shareholder wealth. It sounds simple enough, but things do not always work out so nicely. Even if they are honest and upstanding individuals, directors may sometimes feel a certain degree of obligation to the CEO. The CEO may have even been responsible for having placed them on the board in the first place. Problems arise if the directors are obliged more to the CEO than to the shareholders. When this happens, directors may end up shirking their responsibilities.

Because ownership of publicly traded companies is often spread wide and thin, there may be few—if any—shareholders who have a strong enough incentive to properly monitor the board and the executives. If your investment in a company is worth just a few thousand dollars and represents only a small fraction of your overall net worth, you are not going to expend a great deal of time, effort, or money to make sure the managers are doing what is best for you and all the other owners. Besides, this is what the board of directors is for. You and all the other shareholders rely on the board to act as your watchdog. It is the directors' responsibility to monitor the company and make sure it is being properly managed in your best interest. Furthermore, to a large extent, you can diversify away the risk of being stuck with bad managers by holding shares of other companies in your portfolio as well.

Board Independence

To prevent these kinds of problems, advocates for good corporate governance argue that corporations must have a critical mass of independent directors. Board independence has even become an important issue at the SEC. Under Chairman William Donaldson, the SEC tried to force through a rule requiring that at least 75 percent of a mutual fund's directors—including its chairman—be independent. So far the courts have rejected this proposal. While it may be ridiculous to set an exact number, many governance experts are convinced that when it comes to public corporations, the greater the number of independent directors and the greater their degree of independence, the better.

These experts argue that independent directors are more likely than nonindependent directors to act in the best interests of shareholders. They believe, for example, that independent directors are more likely to exercise proper oversight, which could prevent the company from overpaying the CEO or spending lavishly on perquisites that provide no benefit to shareholders. In addition, independent directors may be more likely to scrutinize proposed business combinations such as mergers and acquisitions. They may be more likely to objectively consider tender offers. And perhaps most important, they may be more likely to question aggressive accounting practices.

Of course, there are plenty of examples of well-run corporations that do not have independent boards. There are also numerous examples of independent boards that failed to prevent companies from getting into trouble. Furthermore, research in this area is not particularly conclusive. When they looked into the matter, economists Sanjai Bhagat and Bernard Black concluded: "There is no convincing evidence that greater board independence correlates with greater firm profitability or faster growth. In particular, there is no empirical support for current proposals that firms should have supermajority-independent boards with only one or two inside directors. To the contrary, there is some evidence that firms with supermajority-independent boards are less profitable than other firms."[1] Research also suggests that the relationship between share performance and board independence is tenuous at best. Nonetheless, corporate governance advocates insist that serious problems such as accounting fraud are less likely to crop up in corporations that have truly independent boards.

Governance experts also argue that the roles of CEO and chairman of the board should be separate and distinct. They say it is a mistake to allow the same person to fill both positions. After all, the CEO reports to the board of directors, and it usually is not a good idea to have the same person in charge of the entity to which he or she reports. In addition, experts say it is crucial for board members to hold at least some meetings without the CEO in the room. They argue that discussions are more likely to be frank and honest when the CEO is not present. This is especially important when the purpose of the meeting is to evaluate the CEO's performance or decide his or her compensation.

Advocates for good corporate governance would be hard-pressed to put their seal of approval on Berkshire Hathaway, a company in which Buffett has served as both chairman and CEO for decades. Furthermore, for almost its entire history, Berkshire's board was anything but independent. Some would argue that even though the board has greater independence today, it still is not independent enough.

An independent board is one with a critical mass of independent directors. According to the Council of Institutional Investors (CII), "an independent director is someone whose only nontrivial professional, familial, or financial connection to the corporation, its chairman, CEO or other executive officer is his or her directorship."[2] Most important, according to the CII, a director cannot be considered independent if during the past five years he or his relatives were employed by the corporation or conducted business with the corporation.

"True" independence may be an ideal that is impossible to achieve. After all, companies want and need qualified directors. This often means high-ranking executives who have significant business experience—preferably in related industries. Chances are such individuals know one another. They may even have engaged in business with one another in the past. Nonetheless, despite the near impossibility of creating a truly independent board, governance advocates insist that corporations should at least try to achieve some minimal level of independence.

Until very recently, however, Berkshire Hathaway could not

make a case that its directors were independent—at least not by the stringent standards established by organizations such as the CII. Of course, Berkshire's shareholders were not complaining. The stock had been doing great for decades. Nonetheless, it has to be said that Buffett and his company were ignoring one of the most important criteria of good governance—at least as stipulated by the so-called experts.

As recently as 2002, Berkshire's board consisted of only seven individuals. Three were named Buffett: Chairman and CEO Warren; his wife, Susan; and their son Howard. Vice Chairman Charles Munger was also on the board. So was Ronald Olson, a partner of the law firm Munger, Tolles & Olson, LLP, which rendered legal advice to Berkshire Hathaway. Chairman of Level 3 Communications Walter Scott, Jr., was on the board. He also had a major investment with Berkshire in MidAmerican Energy Holdings Company. Finally, Malcolm Chace, chairman of BankRI, was on the board. He was a member of the family that owned the textile mills Buffett purchased in 1962. This was the transaction that resulted in the birth of Berkshire Hathaway. Scott and Chace were the only members of Berkshire's board for which a case for independence could be argued; and in Scott's case, you would have had to stretch the definition quite a bit.

Buffett, however, is not keen on how the CII defines independence. He makes an excellent point in Berkshire's 2004 annual report: "The *least* independent directors are likely to be those who receive an important fraction of their income from the fees they receive for board service (and who hope as well to be recommended for election to other boards and thereby to boost their income further). Yet these are the very board members most often classified as 'independent.'"[3] Buffett goes on to explain that such independent directors may make decisions that benefit themselves at the expense of shareholders. For example, an independent director who receives a significant portion of her income from her directorship may oppose a value-maximizing sale of the company if it means losing her directorship and the regular fees that go along with it. Buffett would rather have directors on his board who have a substantial investment in the company because they are the most likely to think like shareholders. In other words, he wants directors who have real skin in the game. He also wants directors who understand the business and who are capable of making important contributions to boardroom discussions, regardless of whether or not they fulfill some expert's arbitrary definition of independence.

While Buffett may be right in his thinking, it must also be said that things at Berkshire are quite different today from what they were just a few short years ago. This is not because Buffett suddenly saw the light and discovered the need for better corporate governance at Berkshire. And it certainly is not because he concluded that the CII's standards were better than his own. Instead, it is because in 2003 the New York Stock Exchange imposed new rules on all listed companies—including Berkshire. In particular, Section 303A of the NYSE's *Listed Company Manual* stipulates that a majority of directors must be independent. The NYSE rules for establishing independence are not nearly as stringent as what the CII recommends, but they are similar. These new rules have forced Berkshire—and many other NYSE listed companies—to significantly alter the structure of their boards.

In response to the new rule, Berkshire increased the number of directors on its board to eleven. Sadly, Susan Buffett passed away in July 2004. Malcolm Chace chose to retire from Berkshire's board in 2007. The remaining five members from the 2002 board are still serving. America's richest man, William (Bill) Gates of

Microsoft fame, is the most interesting of the six new additions to the board. Of course, Gates and Buffett have a well-publicized friendship. You could even say they are members of the same mutual admiration society because they speak so highly of each other. They are both big fans of the card game bridge and they frequently socialize together. But nothing better signifies Buffett's admiration for Gates than his decision to donate $31 billion of his fortune to the Bill & Melinda Gates Foundation, an incredibly magnanimous and selfless gesture by any standard. Yet it also brings to light exactly the kind of relationship that makes advocates of board independence extremely uncomfortable. Despite their misgivings, however, it is probably fair to say, as Berkshire argues in its annual reports, that Bill Gates fits the NYSE's definition of an independent director.

Susan Decker, president of Yahoo!, is the newest and youngest member of Berkshire's board. Interestingly, soon after it was announced that Decker would become a director, rumors broke out that Microsoft was interested in buying Yahoo!. Decker was chosen to replace Malcolm Chace, who decided to retire, citing his age. Chace, who was seventy-two at the time, suggested Berkshire replace him with a younger person. Yet even now there are six members on Berkshire's board, including Buffett, who are older than Chace.

Berkshire claims in its SEC filings that seven of its eleven directors are independent. It includes Scott in this group, despite his continued role at MidAmerican Energy Holdings. Nonetheless, advocates of good governance must admit that Berkshire's current structure is a major improvement over what was an obvious lack of independence just a few years earlier. No matter how they might define independence, they have to admit that Berkshire's board is more independent today than it has ever been in the past.

Here is another important point to ponder: all directors are required to have a substantial stake invested in Berkshire stock. Although the word "substantial" is not defined, Buffett is obviously thinking in absolute—not relative—terms. For example— soon after he joined the board—Bill Gates's investment in Berkshire was valued at about $500 million. That qualifies as substantial by almost any standard, yet it represents less than 1 percent of Gates's net worth.

Berkshire's recent changes in the boardroom are not unique. Spencer Stuart, a major executive search firm that helps corporations find qualified directors, says it has seen a general trend toward greater independence in boardrooms. Much of this is in response to the corporate scandals that resulted in all kinds of new regulations, including the Sarbanes-Oxley Act of 2002 and the previously mentioned NYSE rules.

Interestingly, Spencer Stuart also reports that almost 80 percent of S&P 500 companies have a mandatory retirement age for their directors. The retirement age is commonly set at about seventy years. However, because of what is perceived to be a shortage of qualified independent directors, some companies have increased their mandatory retirement age to seventy-two or older. Some corporate governance advocates favor a mandatory retirement age. They argue that mandatory retirement prevents directors from becoming entrenched and forces the corporation to find new bodies that might bring a different perspective and fresher ideas to the boardroom.

It does seem a little ridiculous, however, to pick some arbitrary age when otherwise valuable and productive board members are forced to step down. Many individuals retain their mental acuity well into their eighties, some into their nineties and beyond. It would make more sense to evaluate directors on an individual basis.

Berkshire has no mandatory retirement age. Indeed, compared to most other large U.S. corporations, the advanced age of many of its directors is highly unusual. Even with Decker replacing Chace, the majority of Berkshire's directors are older than seventy. Four are older than eighty. By no means does this suggest that Berkshire is doing its shareholders a disservice. It does suggest, however, that its heavy reliance on such "experienced" individuals for leadership and direction is unusual even by today's standards.

The Next Buffett

Warren Buffett is a humble man, yet he is also a star. The company's annual meetings are like love-ins. Shareholders travel great distances just to see their idol in person. They hang on his every word. They crowd around him, hoping to shake his hand, get his autograph, or take his picture. Some just want to thank him personally for making them so incredibly wealthy.

Buffett certainly deserves all the adulation. He can truthfully take credit for creating a large number of America's millionaires. Take a look at Figure 7.1 and you will understand why his investors love him so much. Except for a rough patch during the dotcom boom and bust of the late 1990s and early 2000, Berkshire's stock price has been on a rather steady upward trajectory. In fact, for the twenty years ending in 2006, the stock went up about forty times in price. This means a $25,000 investment grew to be worth $1 million in just twenty years. Not even the cost of a college education has kept pace with this kind of appreciation.

Figure 7.1

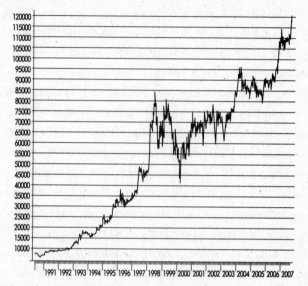

Price Chart for Berkshire Hathaway *(Source: Telemet America)*

Buffett sometimes chastises those who confuse Berkshire's stock purchases with his own. Yet in many investors' minds, Berkshire and Buffett are one and the same. Buffett would disagree, but investors and the media are not necessarily wrong to think this way. After all, Buffett runs Berkshire. He has also said that as much as 99 percent of his personal wealth is invested in Berkshire stock.[4] Because Buffett has been so instrumental in the company's success, it is easy to understand why members of the media sometimes use the words "Buffett" and "Berkshire" interchangeably. It is also understandable why shareholders may be a little anxious about the company's future. Buffett is approaching eighty. While he claims to be in excellent health (which he credits to a diet of Cherry Coke and hamburgers), shareholders know that time waits for no one.

Many investors find it difficult to imagine Berkshire without Buffett. But as each year passes, succession becomes an increasingly important issue. Buffett has big shoes and they will be extremely difficult to fill. Investors want to know who will run Berkshire when Buffett is gone.

For many years, Buffett and Berkshire did not comment on succession plans. But once again the New York Stock Exchange forced Buffett's hand. Section 303A of the NYSE's *Listed Company Manual* mandates the inclusion of "policies regarding succession in the event of an emergency or retirement of the CEO."

Today Berkshire Hathaway has very clear guidelines on corporate governance, including succession planning. According to these guidelines, Buffett regularly discusses succession planning with the board and makes a recommendation on who should replace him in case he is unable to fulfill his responsibilities. The guidelines also say that the board regularly assesses "the strengths and weaknesses of certain individuals currently employed by the Company who could succeed the Chief Executive Officer in the event of his death or disability."[5]

Buffett's 2005 letter to shareholders goes further. In it he states that Berkshire has three relatively young and qualified managers who could easily step into the role of CEO. Buffett says Berkshire's board has assessed each of these three individuals and has unanimously decided on who would succeed him if there was an immediate need. Of course, the directors may change their minds at any time, but at least shareholders know that a concrete plan is in place.

Guessing who might be the next Buffett has become something of a parlor game. Analysts, journalists, and Berkshire shareholders carefully comb through Berkshire's annual reports looking for clues. Buffett has a habit of heaping praise on his managers in his letters. Investors look for those individuals who get the most mentions. They also take note of those who are no longer mentioned. Ajit Jain is a name that frequently pops up. For many years Jain ran Berkshire's National Indemnity insurance unit. More recently, he took over the mega-catastrophe business at Berkshire Hathaway Reinsurance Group. Joe Brandon and Tad Montross also received frequent mentions.[7] Buffett praises them for turning around Berkshire's troubled General Re unit. Although Buffett would probably prefer someone younger, Tony Nicely of GEICO is another individual whose name often surfaces.

Buffett's 2005 letter also reveals another interesting plan. As CEO, Buffett makes both business decisions and investment decisions. But he says there is no single individual who has "my crossover experience that allows me to be comfortable making decisions in either the business arena or in investments."[6] As a result, his replacement will focus only on business. Investment decisions will be made by another individual of the new CEO's choosing. Who might that be? For years, the smart money was betting on Lou Simpson of GEICO. Buffett credits Simpson with making most of Berkshire's investment decisions and said, "Lou is a cinch to be inducted into the investment Hall of Fame."[8] But Simpson would have been a losing bet. Buffett made this clear just two years later. "Lou is a top-notch investor with an outstanding long-term record of managing GEICO's equity portfolio. But he is only six years younger than I. If I were to die soon, he would fill in magnificently for a short period. For the long-term, though, we need a different answer."[9]

Buffett went on to explain that he may hire more than one young candidate who will be trained to take over his investment responsibilities. He is looking for "someone genetically programmed to recognize and avoid serious risks, *including those never before encountered.*"[10] The successful candidate must exhibit "independent thinking, emotional stability, and a keen understanding of both human and institutional behavior."[11] Buffett's remarks resulted in a torrent of résumés. As you can imagine, there are thousands of would-be Buffetts out there who would jump at the opportunity to be trained by the world's greatest investor—and eventually take his job.

No one knows for sure who Buffett's successor will be, but the board has someone waiting in the wings ready to take over operations in case Buffett can no longer fulfill his responsibilities. Plans are also under way to find and train a chief investment officer. In addition, Buffett says the board is ready to act if his mental capabilities begin to slip—even if he may not realize it himself. Buffett has assured his shareholders that Berkshire's board is ready to show him the door when the time comes. He is also trying to assure them that a post-Buffett Berkshire will be just as sound and well managed as it is currently.

KEY TAKEAWAYS: CHAPTER 7

- Corporations with a critical mass of independent directors may be less likely to suffer scandals. However, research suggests there is no relationship between board composition and share price performance. *If you are primarily worried about ending up with a stock like Enron in your portfolio, avoid companies whose boards exhibit little independence. But if you are more concerned about generating good returns over the long run, director independence should not be a major factor in your decision to buy the stock.*

- For decades, Berkshire's board was anything but independent. Yet Berkshire was also one of the best-performing stocks in the market. Berkshire's board is now more independent than it has ever been, but some governance advocates argue it is not independent enough. *Buffett has very high ethical standards. But not all corporations are run by CEOs of Buffett's caliber. Berkshire shareholders may not need to worry much about governance, but for others, governance is a more critical concern.*

- Advocates for good governance insist upon a critical mass of independent directors who have no meaningful professional, familial, or financial ties to the corporation, its chairman, CEO, or other executive officers. Buffett disagrees. He says a truly independent director is one who thinks like a shareholder and has a significant financial stake in the company. Furthermore, the income the director earns from director fees should represent only a small fraction of his or her total income. *Read the proxy statement to find out how much stock each director owns. So-called independent directors who have little invested in the company are not likely to provide much value to the corporation and its shareholders.*

- Succession planning is especially critical when a company's success is so closely tied to a single individual. Investors are right to worry about Berkshire's future after Buffett. But Berkshire has strong succession plans in place. *You should be wary of investing in a company with a "star" CEO unless the board is transparent about succession plans.*

8

No Options for Buffett

My successor at Berkshire may well receive much of his pay via options.

—Warren Buffett, 2004

Thanks largely to headline-making corporate scandals and bankruptcies such as Enron and WorldCom, employee stock options became a hotly debated issue. In truth, few of the scandals had much to do with options. Most were related to some kind of accounting fraud. But investors and policymakers came to view options as a symbol of the kind of greed that had driven executive compensation to stratospheric levels. Warren Buffett in particular has been one of the most vocal critics of excessive CEO compensation.

To appreciate how CEO compensation has changed over the years, all you have to do is compare what CEOs make to what the average worker makes. James Reda is a leading independent compensation and corporate governance consultant. He also authored the *Compensation Committee Handbook,* a guidebook used by directors at some of the largest U.S. corporations who are assigned the task of determining how and how much CEOs should be paid. According to Reda, back in the 1970s, the typical CEO made approximately twenty to twenty-five times what the average employee made. By the early 2000s, however, this multiple ballooned to about four hundred. Much of the increase was due to stock options and other long-term incentives.

Few investors complained about CEO compensation when stock prices were going straight up during the bull market of the 1990s. As long as share prices were rising they were happy. But when the stock market boom ended and huge paper gains turned into significant losses, investors wanted something done about excessive CEO pay. They were particularly irked when CEOs made tens of millions or more even while stock prices were falling. Not even nonprofit organizations escaped the backlash.

Richard Grasso, CEO of the New York Stock Exchange (which was a nonprofit at the time), was considered a hero for getting the Big Board quickly back in business after the September 11 terrorist attacks. But he came under severe criticism when it was revealed that he had received a deferred compensation package worth approximately $140 million. Thanks largely to stock options, however, some of the leading titans in the corporate sector were making even more. Even lackluster executives who were forced out of their jobs walked away with eight- and sometimes nine-figure severance packages.

There is no denying that stock options were severely abused during the stock market boom. Some companies handed out options like candy—especially to C-level executives (e.g., CEOs and CFOs). Others canceled existing options when stock prices fell and immediately replaced them with new ones with much lower exercise prices—a practice commonly referred to as *repricing*. Worse still, some companies simply lied about the grant dates. Instead of being truthful about the actual grant date, they chose a date from the past when the stock price was at a lower and more favorable level—a practice known as *backdating*. Backdating, however, did not come to light until many years after the boom ended. Although some experts claim backdating options is simply another legitimate form of compensation, former SEC chairman Harvey Pitt calls backdating outright fraud.[1]

Some commentators called for a ban on stock options altogether. Others, including Warren Buffett, concluded that mandatory expensing of options was the proper solution to the abuse. Most companies were not including the implied cost of stock options as an expense on their income statements. That's because they did not have to. Back in 1994, when Congress was debating the issue, it decided to give companies an option of their own. Companies could either expense employee stock options on the income statement, or they could simply state the estimated value of these options in the footnotes to the financial statements. Because expensing options reduces reported earnings, it did not take a rocket scientist to figure out which option CEOs and CFOs would choose.

To appreciate the intricacies of this issue, it is imperative to understand what an option really is. An option is nothing but a right. Specifically, it gives the owner the right (but not the obligation) to buy the stock at a set price by some particular date. Listed options trade on an exchange. Any investor can buy or sell them. Employee stock options, however, do not trade. They are granted to a particular individual and ownership is not transferable. Employee stock options also have much longer expiration dates than exchange traded options. They typically do not expire for ten years and they vest over time.

Everyone agrees employee stock options have value when they

are granted. But problems arise when you try to determine exactly how much an option is worth. That's because no one knows if the company's stock price will rise or by how much. Furthermore, even if this valuation hurdle can be overcome, there is disagreement on when, if ever, the option should be expensed.

What Is an Option Worth?

Several decades ago, three scholars, Fischer Black, Myron Scholes, and Robert Merton, began work on trying to determine how much stock options are worth. Of course, the market price of an exchange traded option can be observed. It is what the last buyer was willing to pay for it, or what the last seller was willing to take. But these economists wanted to know what an option was worth in theory. Their work required an understanding of higher-level mathematics. Amazingly, they derived a formula that turned out to be the solution to the heat-exchange equation from physics. Dubbed the Black-Scholes option pricing model, it does an excellent job of valuing at-the-money exchange traded options that trade frequently and are relatively short-lived.

However, theoretical pricing models such as Black-Scholes do not work particularly well when it comes to valuing nontradable employee stock options that do not expire for many years. Furthermore, the Black-Scholes model requires the use of something known as the stock's *instantaneous standard deviation* (a measure of volatility). This variable is difficult enough to comprehend, let alone estimate. Indeed, critics sometimes accuse certain corporations of intentionally lowballing their estimate for this variable in order to minimize the option's derived value and its impact on earnings.

Corporations disclose the computed value of their employee stock options in Form 10-K, which they file annually with the SEC. They also describe how the calculations were made. These descriptions can be extremely convoluted and confusing. For example, Honeywell's 10-K talks about the Black-Scholes model, implied volatilities, Monte Carlo simulation, and the U.S. Treasury yield curve. But there is nothing particularly unusual about Honeywell. This kind of description is found in the 10-K of any major corporation that issues employee stock options.

The point is that valuing employee stock options is extremely difficult. Despite the near impossibility of deriving an accurate value, Buffett argued in a 2002 *Washington Post* op-ed that difficulty in determining the value of an option should not prevent us from making a reasonable estimate. He pointed out that accountants estimate the cost of lots of things, including the useful life of machinery for depreciation purposes.[2]

However, depreciation is not an appropriate analogy. When a corporation buys a piece of machinery, it knows the exact cost to the penny. There may be some uncertainty about how much of that cost should be expensed in any given year, but there is no uncertainty about the actual cost.

But with options, the corporation is merely guessing at the cost. When the option is granted, its cost cannot be determined with any degree of certainty. In fact, the actual cost of the option will not be known until years later, when the employee actually exercises his or her right to buy the stock. And if for some reason the option is never exercised—for example, because the stock price doesn't rise—there is no cost.

Yet Buffett eloquently argued in his *Washington Post* op-ed that options are a form of compensation, that compensation is an expense, and that an expense should go into the calculation of earnings. This logic is classic Buffett—simple, to the point, and very convincing. Reality, however, is more complicated.

Consider this example: Suppose you accept a job at a small company with a promising future. The going annual salary for this position is $100,000. However, the hiring manager explains that cash flow is tight, so instead of paying you the going rate, you will be paid only $90,000. To make up the difference, you will also receive 1,000 stock options exercisable at the current market price of $20 per share.

Thanks largely to Buffett and his allies who successfully petitioned Congress after the stock market meltdown in 2000, accounting rules were changed. As a result, companies now must estimate how much options are worth when they are granted, and they must expense that full amount on the income statement as the options vest. It is no longer enough to simply disclose this estimated value in the footnotes to the financial statements. Suppose that by using the Black-Scholes model or some other theoretical approach your new employer determines that the 1,000 options you were granted are worth $5 each. As a result, the company expenses $5,000 on the income statement.

Now suppose you and all the other employees work very hard and the company becomes extremely successful. Let's assume the stock price goes all the way up to $100 per share just a few years after you accepted the job and received your options. Since the options give you the right to buy the stock at $20 per share, you are in an enviable position. When you exercise the options, you pay the company $20,000 and receive 1,000 shares of common stock in return. Because the stock is selling for $100 per share, you can immediately sell your newly acquired shares for $100,000.

Your profit before taxes is $80,000, which more than makes up for the lower salary you had accepted when you took the job. Sounds like a great deal, doesn't it?

There are a couple of problems with this approach. First, what the company expensed and what those options actually ended up costing the company are two different things. The true economic cost of those options is the difference between the market value of the shares and what you actually paid for them. The company could have sold those 1,000 shares in the market to someone else for $100,000. Instead, it sold them to you for only $20,000. Therefore, your $80,000 profit represents an opportunity cost to the company and all the other shareholders. Of course, this was offset somewhat by the savings the company realized by paying you a lower salary for all those years.

Furthermore, even if there is an opportunity cost, it is not necessarily a cash cost. If the company gave you Treasury stock, or stock that was authorized but not yet issued, no cash left the company. In fact, just the opposite occurred. The company's cash flow increased by $20,000 when you exercised your options. However, if the company had to purchase the shares in the open market for $100 each before handing them over to you for $20, there is a real $80,000 cash outflow. In any case, if the stock price goes up by a considerable amount, the company's valuation of those options at the time they were issued might understate the true cost of those options.

A completely different problem arises if the options are never exercised. Suppose you quit your job after your options vest but for some reason you don't exercise them. Or suppose you remain in your position but the company falters and the stock price falls. Now your options expire worthless. Even though the company expensed $5,000 when it granted those options to you, the options end up costing the company nothing. In fact, it could be argued that your employer actually saved $10,000 per year because you agreed to work for an annual salary of $90,000 instead of $100,000. Yet under current accounting rules, the company can't reverse that $5,000 charge. In this case, what the company expensed overstates the true cost of the options.

The ironic thing is that when the stock price falls, the true cost of an option is less than what was actually expensed. But when the stock price rises, the true cost could be much greater. Yet if the stock price goes up, all the shareholders are better off—not just the employees who were granted options.

What really rankles investors is when executives exercise their options right after the stock runs up and then sell their shares just before the stock falls back down. This was a pattern that played out over and over during the stock market boom and bust of the late 1990s and early 2000s. There are some who oppose the use of stock options entirely because they believe options give executives an incentive to manipulate prices or to take on projects that are too risky. For example, executives might try to hide bad news to keep their options in the money. Or they might resort to accounting gimmicks to artificially inflate the stock price—at least until they can exercise their options, sell the shares, and reap their ill-gotten gains.

The Real Problem Is Abuse

In the example above, the company expensed $5,000. But as we saw, if the stock price climbed to $100, the true cost of those options was much higher. Economists Burton Malkiel and William Baumol argue in a 2002 *Wall Street Journal* op-ed that even though it may be accurate to expense options when they are exercised, it is also perverse, because the higher the stock price goes, the bigger will be the hit to earnings.[3] This is not to say that Malkiel and Baumol favor expensing options on the grant date. They do not. They stress that the real problem is the abuse of options, something expensing will not solve. They express a fear that expensing options will simply discourage their use. Malkiel and Baumol suggest using performance-based options that are properly structured.

Similarly, entrepreneurs John Doerr and Frederick Smith argue in a 2002 *New York Times* op-ed that options should not be expensed.[4] They explain that corporations already report diluted earnings per share. This figure is computed by dividing net income by shares outstanding, assuming options are exercised. Therefore, expensing options in addition to treating them as shares outstanding amounts to double-counting, which distorts reported earnings by understating their true amount. Doerr and Smith also argue that expensing options discourages their use, making it more difficult for corporations to secure talent and align the interests of employees and owners.

Buffett, however, did not buy these arguments. Buffett was convinced that expensing options would go a long way in solving many of the abuse-related problems. He also did not believe that expensing options would discourage their use. However, because Buffett was so vocal about this issue, there is a widespread perception in the investment community that he despises options. Many investors believe that Buffett's real goal was to eliminate the use of options altogether. He is the CEO of one of the largest companies in America, yet he has never received options himself. Furthermore, the media has rarely quoted him as saying anything nice about options.

The reality, however, is quite different. Buffett does not oppose the use of stock options. In fact, he says, "Because the attempts to obfuscate the stock-option issue continue, it's worth pointing out that no one—neither the FASB [Financial Accounting Standards Board], nor investors generally, nor I—are talking about restricting the use of options in any way."[5] He continues, "My successor at Berkshire may well receive much of his pay via options."[6]

Many observers are surprised to hear this. The fact is that Buffett believes options can be an appropriate form of incentive compensation as long as they are properly structured. While he does oppose the use of options that have a fixed exercise price, he has no objection to employing options with an exercise price that adjusts periodically to reflect changes in retained earnings. If the exercise price is fixed, executives might be rewarded simply for being on the job during a bull market. A floating exercise price, however, properly rewards executives for creating value.

Buffett would also like to see restrictions imposed on when executives can sell shares. He argues it is wrong to allow them to sell immediately after acquiring the shares through the exercise of options. After all, once they have sold the stock, they have lost the incentive to think and act like owners. Forcing employees to hold on to the stock after they exercise their options sounds perfectly logical, but it is a more complicated issue than it appears. This is because exercising an option triggers a tax liability. Employees often sell the shares in order to pay the tax. If we are going to impose restrictions on their ability to sell, it would only be fair for the IRS to adjust the way it taxes this event. First, it should postpone the tax until after the shares are actually sold. Second, it should take into consideration any gain or loss that occurs in the stock price after the options are exercised. Indeed, many loyal employees with good intentions learned an extremely expensive lesson back in the early 2000s when stock prices were falling. They held on to their shares after exercising their options, just as Buffett favors. But they got burned when stock prices fell. Some ended up with a tax liability that exceeded the value of their shares.

Buffett's proposals on how to properly structure options make a great deal of sense. Corporate boards would be well advised to listen to his suggestions. Many of Buffett's proposals would no doubt go a long way in reducing abuse. However, his insistence that options be expensed when granted is not as logical. As we saw earlier in this chapter, many experts are convinced that expensing options when granted not only reduces the accuracy of reported earnings; it also discourages the use of options altogether.

As Buffett explains, there is nothing wrong with rewarding employees with options. Stock options are a perfectly appropriate and effective form of compensation. They do indeed go a long way in aligning the interests of employees and shareholders. After all, the more skin employees have in the game, the more likely they are to think like shareholders, and the more focused they will be on working hard to ensure the company's success and see its stock price rise—not just in the short term, but over the long term as well.

Buffett is also right to complain about options-related abuses. Making excessive grants to favored executives, repricing options after stock prices fall, backdating options to obtain more favorable exercise prices, and a host of other abuses that are not readily transparent are all wrong. Some are illegal.

Buffett has also criticized another form of abuse that is often overlooked: share buybacks (or *repurchases,* as they are often called). This will no doubt come as a surprise to many investors since they typically welcome buybacks. In general, Buffett agrees that corporations should return cash to shareholders when managers can't find value-maximizing projects in which to invest. Returning cash to investors can be achieved either through dividends or buybacks. When management is convinced that the stock is selling below its intrinsic value, buybacks make perfect sense. However, Buffett warns that the use of stock options to compensate employees gives executives a perverse incentive to favor buybacks even when the stock is overvalued. This is because buybacks can boost the stock price further by decreasing the number of shares outstanding and increasing earnings per share. By initiating a buyback, executives can actually boost the value of their options.

But Buffett was wrong about the impact of expensing options on the frequency of their use. The fact is that corporations began issuing fewer stock options soon after regulators required that options be expensed, just as many economists had predicted. No doubt some observers applaud this outcome. They should not. For large, profitable companies, expensing options is not a big deal. At most, it might erase a few pennies per share from reported earnings. Furthermore, large corporations can use alternative means to compensate their employees. They can usually afford to give them more cash and fewer options. However, expensing options is problematic for many small corporations, especially start-ups that are not yet profitable and have little cash flow to begin with. In the past, these smaller companies relied heavily on stock options to entice and retain the most talented workers. Now that options must be expensed, they are having a more difficult time recruiting the best talent.

The jury is still out on this issue. Mandatory expensing of stock options appears to have reduced the abuse, but it has also made options a less common form of remuneration. Today both large and small companies are seeking alternative ways to incentivize and compensate employees. Only time will tell if expensing turns out to be the panacea its proponents claim it is, or just a new kind of snake oil that ends up killing the enthusiasm of America's most innovative entrepreneurs.

KEY TAKEAWAYS: CHAPTER 8

- Excessive executive compensation is a hot-button issue. Many of the huge gains reaped by CEOs and other executives have come from stock options and other kinds of incentives. *To find out how much the top executives at any public corporation are getting paid, go to www.sec.gov and look for Form DEF 14A (a.k.a. the proxy). You should avoid investing in companies that provide excessive amounts of compensation to top executives.*

- The Black-Scholes option pricing model does a good job of coming up with a theoretical value for at-the-money exchange traded options that are short lived. It does not work as well for valuing nontradable employee options that might not expire for years. Despite this shortcoming, the model is commonly used for that purpose. *Look in the 10-K to find out how much the options are worth and what methodology was used to estimate that value. Avoid companies if quarterly options-related expenses amount to more than just a few pennies per share.*

- Following the dot-com bust, Buffett and his allies convinced regulators to require the expensing of stock options when they are granted. Buffett hoped this mandate would put an end to the abuse. Indeed, options-related compensation abuse does appear to have decreased in recent years. The trade-off, however, is that options are being used less frequently. This trend has made it particularly difficult for start-ups with little cash flow to attract the best workers. *Accounting rules requiring the expensing of options give large, well-capitalized companies a comparative advantage over small start-ups. To take advantage of this development, consider raising your portfolio's allocation to large-cap stocks.*

- Companies issue fewer options these days, but that was not Buffett's intention. In fact, Buffett believes options are a perfectly appropriate tool for compensating senior-level executives as long as they are properly structured. Furthermore, he favors restricting the sale of stock acquired by exercising options. *Look for companies that issue options with floating exercise prices and other characteristics that properly reward executives for creating value. Also, favor companies that have some sort of restriction on the sale of shares acquired by exercising options.*

9

The Pro-Tax Buffett

I came wired at birth with a talent for capital allocation.
—Warren Buffett, 2003

Warren Buffett has proven again and again his ability to create tremendous wealth—not just for himself, but for all of Berkshire's shareholders. Indeed, he is personally responsible for creating a large number of millionaires. As we have seen, Buffett is also a vocal critic of CEO greed and has a reputation for sticking up for shareholder rights. Yet we have also seen that Buffett sometimes takes positions on issues that do investors more harm than good. Perhaps the most glaring example is his call for higher taxes. Buffett favors higher income taxes on the so-called rich as well as higher estate taxes.

A Necessary Evil

Well-functioning governments rely on taxes to pay for all kinds of things that benefit every member of society. Taxes pay for the military to defend the homeland and for the police to safeguard the streets. Taxes pay for public education systems, roads, and bridges. Taxes also pay for all the social programs that provide aid to the poor, disabled, and otherwise needy.

Regardless of their political views, all but anarchists agree that taxes are necessary. They also agree that everyone should pay their "fair" share. But problems arise when they get down to the particulars. What exactly is fair? How high should tax rates be? What exactly should be taxed?

As far as income goes, liberals argue that those who make more money should not just pay more tax; they should also pay a greater proportion of their income in tax. In other words, they believe tax rates should be much higher for those who have larger incomes. Liberals favor progressive tax rates.

Conservatives counter that if income tax rates are flat, those who make more will pay more. Conservatives object strongly to progressive tax rates, which they say are inherently unfair and cause harm to the economy by reducing the incentive to work hard and be productive. They also argue that progressive tax rates discourage investment. While these detrimental effects may not be very noticeable if rates are only mildly progressive, excessively progressive tax rates can slow economic growth, result in fewer jobs being created, and generate *less* revenue for the government.

Many noted conservative economists, entrepreneurs, and politicians, including Milton Friedman, Steve Forbes, and Dick Armey, have long advocated a simplified and flat tax system. They also favor eliminating loopholes and deductions that allow those who can afford to hire clever accountants to escape paying their fair share. They are convinced that a simple and flat tax code would spur economic activity *and* increase government revenues at the same time.

There is plenty of evidence that economies thrive when tax rates are low. Russia, for example, experienced strong economic growth and a surge in tax revenues shortly after implementing a simplified and low flat tax. Even in the United States, economic growth accelerated and tax revenues increased to record levels shortly after the George W. Bush tax cuts went into effect.[1]

Liberals complain that the highest earners need to pay more tax because they get such a large share of aggregate income. Conservatives counter that they already pay most of the taxes. According to the Internal Revenue Service, the top 1 percent of earners accounted for 21 percent of total adjusted gross income in 2005, but they also paid 39 percent of all individual taxes collected that year. The top quarter, which accounted for 68 percent of total adjusted gross income, paid 86 percent of all individual income taxes. The bottom 50 percent, which received 13 percent of all the income, hardly paid any tax at all. Their share of total taxes came out to just 3 percent. To conservatives, this proves the tax code is too progressive. To liberals, it proves it isn't progressive enough.

Buffett's 3 Percent Tax Rate

It may seem a bit odd that Warren Buffett, one of the greatest capitalists the world has ever seen, resides firmly in the liberal camp when it comes to tax policy. Buffett favors higher taxes on both income and wealth. His writings call for higher income taxes at the corporate level and more progressive income taxes at the personal level.

In his 2003 letter to shareholders, Buffett stated that Berkshire was about to make a $3.3 billion tax payment, or 2.5 percent of all corporate taxes paid to the U.S. Treasury that year. Buffett said Berkshire was "among the country's top ten taxpayers." He went on to complain that because of various tax breaks, corporations paid only 7.4 percent of all federal receipts in 2003. He also pointed out that back in 1952 the corporate share of tax receipts was 32 percent. Buffett's point is that corporations in general are carrying less of the tax burden while individuals are carrying more. Buffett also made a strong—but perhaps unintentional—case for tax simplification. He said Berkshire's tax return for the previous year (2002) totaled 8,905 pages.[2]

By 2006, Berkshire's federal tax burden had grown to $4.4 billion. Its tax return that year amounted to 9,386 pages.[3] You might imagine it would require a vast bureaucracy to handle this much paperwork. But as Buffett points out, Berkshire has just nineteen employees on staff at its headquarters, occupying only ten thousand square feet of office space. And total annual payroll, including benefits, is just $3.5 million. That figure includes both Buffett's and Munger's salaries of $100,000 each.

The government is no doubt grateful that Berkshire pays so much tax. Berkshire's shareholders, however, should be at least a little concerned. As Buffett said, Berkshire's federal tax bill amounted to 2.5 percent of all taxes collected in 2003. But Berkshire made only 1.2 percent of total corporate income that year. In other words, Berkshire appears to be paying much more than its fair share of taxes.

Yet Buffett seems proud that Berkshire generates so much money—and so efficiently—for the government. And although he thinks individual taxpayers carry too much of the overall tax burden, in a *Washington Post* op-ed dated May 20, 2003, Buffett took the Senate to task for passing a bill that would have eliminated individual taxes on dividend income. Buffett argued that the bill would benefit no one but the rich. Although Berkshire pays no dividends, Buffett pointed out that if the dividend tax were eliminated and Berkshire were to implement a $1 billion dividend, he personally would receive $310 million tax free. He said this would drive his personal tax rate all the way down to 3 percent. He also warned that the enactment of sunset dates in the Senate's proposal amounted to "Enron-style accounting," which would result in no dividends being paid until the tax was eliminated, and a flood of dividends being paid immediately thereafter.[4]

Of course, corporations can do one of several things with their cash. They can simply sit on it, perhaps investing it in low-yielding marketable securities. This is usually not a good idea, however, because it will depress the stock price. They can reinvest the cash—into projects intended to earn a high enough rate of return to increase the stock price. They can repurchase shares, which returns cash in the form of capital gains to those shareholders who choose to sell their shares. Or they can pay a dividend, which returns cash to all shareholders in the form of ordinary income.

Finance theory says that when management is unable to find wealth-maximizing projects to invest in, it should return the cash to shareholders. How it does that—whether through share repurchases or dividends—can be influenced by a number of factors, including prevailing tax rates. If ordinary income is taxed at substantially higher rates than capital gains, as was the case prior to the Bush tax reforms, buybacks are the preferred route. But if the tax rate on dividends is lower than it is on capital gains, dividends would be the better choice for shareholders.

Despite the Senate's efforts, taxes on dividends were not eliminated. However, when President Bush finally signed the Jobs and Growth Tax Relief Reconciliation Act of 2003, the maximum tax rates on dividends and long-term (i.e., longer than a year) capital gains were both lowered to 15 percent. Those like Buffett who oppose lower taxes on dividends ignore the fact that dividends have already been taxed at the corporate level. This is the "double taxation" investors and economists often complain about. Many economists argue that corporate income should be taxed only once. If corporations pay the tax, individuals should not have to pay an additional tax. However, if individuals pay the tax, then corporations should not pay a tax in the first place.

Berkshire's directors made a wise decision not to pay a dividend in 2003. Unlike interest payments on debt, which are tax-deductible, dividend payments must be made from a corporation's after-tax income. U.S. tax laws do not allow corporations to deduct dividend payments for tax purposes. Therefore, if Berkshire had paid a dividend in 2003, there would have been absolutely no effect on its $3.3 billion tax bill. However, by paying a dividend, Berkshire would have forced its shareholders to pay an additional tax. If for some reason they really wanted to return cash to investors, it would have been better to initiate a share repurchase. Although the shareholders would have been taxed on their gains, the tax would have been less onerous than if they had received dividends. However, tax rates for individuals on both dividends and capital gains have since been reduced to 15 percent. As a result, returning cash to shareholders today would do them less harm from a tax perspective than it would have back in 2003. Furthermore, since dividend income and capital gains are currently taxed at the same rate, there is little advantage of one over the other.[5]

Buffett Favors Death Tax, Yet Avoids It

Unlike income taxes, the estate tax is based on wealth. Liberals refer to it as the "wealth tax." They argue it is right for the government to confiscate wealth from those who have substantial estates soon after they pass on. After all, as the argument goes, the privilege of living in America is what made them rich in the first place. Instead of simply passing on their wealth to the next generation, the wealthy should be forced to relinquish a large chunk of their treasure to the government once they die.

This kind of thinking equates wealth to luck. Those who think this way believe luck is the most significant factor explaining the difference between the rich and poor. Even Buffett credits luck for much of his success. He says he was lucky to have been born in America and even luckier that "I came wired at birth with a talent for capital allocation."[6]

Conservatives, on the other hand, refer to the estate tax as the "death tax." They object to the government confiscating someone's estate simply because he or she died. They point out that wealth is what is left over after taxes have been paid. It would be wrong to tax that wealth over and over again. Conservatives stress that a death tax punishes hard work and frugality, and encourages wastefulness and spendthrift behavior. After all, if you know the government is going to take a large chunk of whatever you leave behind, why not try to spend as much of it as you can before you go? Why invest your wealth and try to create more? Why save anything if you know you can't leave it to your loved ones?

In addition, conservatives argue that wealth is not always liquid. Just because someone might have a large estate, it does not mean it is all piled up nicely under the mattress or sitting in a savings account at the local bank. Some of it might be in stocks and bonds, but a good chunk might be invested in hard assets that are needed to run a business. Taxing wealth could force the business to shut down because it has to sell assets to raise cash to pay the government. One might literally have to sell the proverbial farm in order to pay the estate tax. Conservatives say it would be wiser to allow the heirs to continue running the business. The government, after all, will get its due by taxing the income the business produces.

Nobel laureate Milton Friedman was a vocal critic of the estate tax. He called it an immoral tax that punishes virtue, discourages saving, and encourages wasteful spending.[7] He even questioned its value as a source of revenue for the government. He argued that the government spends more money each year trying to collect the tax than the tax actually brings in. This is because estate planners have devised clever ways to allow their wealthy clients to avoid paying the tax. By eliminating the estate tax—and all the loopholes it has given birth to—Friedman believed the government would actually generate greater net revenues.

Singer Pat Boone, who also serves as spokesman for the 60 Plus Association, even went so far as to accuse Buffett in *The Washington Times* of personally benefiting from the estate tax.[8] He said Berkshire had purchased a business that profited from selling estate tax insurance. This kind of insurance policy makes sure that heirs have enough money available to pay the estate tax without having to liquidate assets. Indeed, one estimate says that "as much as 10% of life insurance sales are related to estate-tax planning."[9]

Several members of the megarich class, including Buffett, George Soros, and William Gates, Sr. (Bill Gates's father), opposed efforts by the Bush administration in 2001 to eliminate the estate tax. Gates testified in Congress and expressed concern that eliminating the estate tax would reduce charitable donations. After all, he seemed to argue, if there is no estate tax, there is no need to escape it by giving away your money.

Although there is little empirical evidence linking charitable contributions to a motivation to avoid taxes, giving away your fortune before you die is one sure way to avoid the estate tax. In

2004, *The Wall Street Journal* suggested to Buffett that he should make sure his money would go to the government if he felt so strongly about the need for an estate tax. The *Journal* challenged him not to take advantage of the loophole in estate-tax laws by donating his wealth to a foundation before his death.[10] However, as everyone knows by now, this is exactly what Buffett did when he pledged to give $31 billion to the Bill & Melinda Gates Foundation and another $6 billion to foundations run by his children.[11]

Buffett firmly believes the rich should pay more tax. So why would he choose to give so much of his money to these various foundations rather than allow the government to take a huge chunk from his estate after his death? The only reasonable explanation is that Buffett is convinced that these foundations will spend his money much more wisely than the government would.

Many of the megarich, including Buffett, favor the estate tax. Yet they continue to take advantage of the loophole in the law that allows them to avoid the tax by giving their money away before they die. What explains this paradox? Perhaps the answer lies somewhere between guilt and altruism. They may feel guilty about having so much money, yet they don't trust the government to spend it wisely. But as conservatives point out, we don't need an estate tax to get the same result. Those who feel guilty are free to give their money to whomever they want—even the government. But they should not force the same on others.

KEY TAKEAWAYS: CHAPTER 9

- In recent years, some of the best investment opportunities have arisen in countries that are transforming their economies. Russia and China, for example, are moving toward free-market capitalism and away from state control. *Allocate a portion of your portfolio to emerging economies. The easiest way to do this is with mutual funds and exchange traded funds.*

- Although taxes are a necessary evil, how they are structured is critical to the health of the economy. Taxes that are too high or excessively progressive discourage investment. *Allocate a greater proportion of your portfolio to stocks during periods when tax rates are being cut and when the tax code is becoming less progressive. Allocate less when Congress is pushing tax hikes.*

- When it comes to taxes, Buffett leans decidedly toward the liberal camp. He opposed congressional efforts to eliminate taxes on dividend income. Congress, however, lowered tax rates on both dividends and long-term capital gains to 15 percent. Unless these cuts become permanent, tax rates will revert to higher levels in 2011. Although Buffett favors higher taxes, he agrees that such sunset clauses are ridiculous. *Unless there is good reason to hope that tax rates will not be increased, get ready to reduce your allocation to equities as we approach 2011. In particular, be prepared to pare down on the highest dividend yielding stocks since they will be taxed at the highest rates.*

- Buffett also opposed efforts to eliminate the estate tax. He sides with liberals who say that living in America is what allowed the rich to become rich in the first place. Therefore, once they pass on, their wealth should go to the government. Conservatives, however, point out that wealth is created from hard work and frugality. It is what is left over after taxes have been paid. Therefore, it should not be taxed again. The estate tax is due to expire in 2010, then return with a vengeance in 2011. *If you expect to leave an estate worth at least $1 million in 2011 or later, make sure you get good estate planning advice. Also, consider following Buffett's lead. Take advantage of loopholes that allow you to avoid or minimize the estate tax by donating your wealth to the foundation of your choice before you die.*

10

Give Us Guidance

Based on our evidence, we cannot endorse the frequently voiced recommendation to firms to cease providing quarterly guidance.
—Joel Houston, Baruch Lev, Jenny Tucker, 2007

In chapter 4 we learned that Buffett openly admits that his refusal to sell a good business at any price hurts Berkshire's financial performance. We learned in chapter 9 that Buffett's opposition to lower taxes on the so-called rich does not serve the best interests of investors. In this chapter we will find out that Buffett is also a critic of earnings guidance. Indeed, he has encouraged several companies in Berkshire's portfolio, including Coca-Cola, The Washington Post, and Gillette, to stop providing guidance. His opposition to guidance is another example of how his views can harm investors.

Earnings guidance refers to management's practice of telling investors and analysts how much they should expect the corporation to earn in future reporting periods. Guidance is usually conveyed during a conference call or in a press release. Over the years, Buffett became convinced that guidance is a bad thing. He believes that it inappropriately encourages managers and investors to focus on short-run profits rather than long-run results. Instead of

giving specific earnings guidance, Buffett and his ilk say that corporations should provide more details about the business. They
should tell investors more about the key metrics that are important in the industry, and disclose more information about the
company's long-term strategies.

To really understand why guidance is so controversial, it is first
necessary to understand how earnings are reported in the United
States. The SEC requires every public corporation to file a quarterly earnings report called a 10-Q. It also requires companies to
file an annual earnings report called a 10-K. The annual filing
must be audited by a public accounting firm, but the quarterly
filings are not audited. The purpose of these reports is to provide
shareholders—the owners—with information about how their
company is doing. The 10-K is audited so shareholders can have
some confidence that management is not simply making up the
numbers.

Corporations must report actual earnings, but there is no requirement for them to provide guidance about future earnings. In
other words, management must tell investors exactly how much
the company earned in the past, but it is under no obligation to
discuss how much the company might earn in the future. Nonetheless, most companies voluntarily choose to comment on future
expectations often by providing specific earnings projections.
Their reasons for doing so vary, but it basically boils down to one
thing: investors demand the information. This is the same reason
that many companies chose to voluntarily report actual financial
results on a quarterly basis long before the SEC required them to
do so.[1]

If a company earns a lot of money in the most recently completed quarter, that is all well and good. But what investors really
want to know is what to expect in the future. After all, the price

of a stock discounts future expectations—not past results. The past is history. It may be interesting and it may give us a sense of comfort, but the past is relevant only if it tells us something useful about the future. In particular, do past results indicate that recent trends will continue, or is there reason to think things will change dramatically?

Investors who buy shares today have no right to the cash flows that were distributed in the past. They have rights only to future cash flows. This is why investors want to hear about the future. This is why they want to know what to expect. Skeptics, however, say that individual investors are not the ones who are demanding this information. They say it is really the analysts and the institutional investors who are requesting guidance. They cite numbers indicating that individual investors are becoming a shrinking part of the overall market while institutions such as mutual funds, pension funds, insurance companies, and hedge funds are accounting for an increasing proportion of share ownership and trading activity. They say it is naïve to argue that ordinary investors want guidance.

There is some truth to this argument, but it is entirely irrelevant. It suggests that only individual investors are worth worrying about. It implies that we should not care about the presumably more sophisticated class of institutional investors. However, institutions represent individuals. Behind every institutional investor is a group of individual investors. Why should it matter if you own shares of General Electric directly or indirectly through a mutual fund or pension fund? Either way, your overall financial well-being depends on how well GE stock does. Therefore, it makes no sense to argue that institutions and individuals are entirely distinct entities with disparate investment interests.

Manage for the Long Run

Yet even if they do not rail against institutions, critics claim that earnings guidance improperly forces corporate executives to manage the company for the short run rather than the long run. They argue that guidance causes executives to manage earnings rather than the business. They seem to believe that by eliminating guidance, management will magically shift its focus to doing what benefits shareholders in the long run rather than simply trying to beat earnings expectations in the current quarter.

There is no question that it is better to manage with a long-term horizon in mind. Short-run earnings management is clearly a bad idea. For example, management can easily boost earnings in the current quarter simply by cutting expenditures on research and development. Doing so, however, may depress earnings next year. Indeed, it could potentially depress earnings for several years. Obviously, this would not be a smart decision, even if it causes a significant but temporary spike in the stock price.

Such earnings manipulation may indeed be the result of pressure to "meet the number." Yet that pressure is not caused by guidance. Whether management provides guidance or not, the simple fact is that analysts and investors will continue to form expectations. Because the SEC requires quarterly earnings reports, investors will form quarterly expectations. If the SEC required corporations to report financial earnings every month, investors would form monthly expectations. There is absolutely no escaping this simple and fundamental fact.

Since guidance is not what causes investors to form expectations, it makes no sense to encourage companies to stop providing it. On the contrary, eliminating guidance is likely to make matters worse. After all, guidance from management is perhaps the most reliable source of information investors can obtain about future earnings. Guidance comes from those who are actually running the company—straight from the horse's mouth. No one could possibly know better than management what the corporation is likely to earn. Eliminating this critical source of information will merely increase the level of uncertainty.

What We Really Hate Is Volatility

Buffett and others who oppose guidance are no doubt convinced they are doing what is best for shareholders. But it seems what they are most upset about is the tremendous stock price volatility that so commonly accompanies corporations' earnings announcements. It is not uncommon, for example, to see a company's share price fall by several dollars simply because it missed the consensus earnings estimate by a few pennies. Opponents to guidance who rightly prefer a focus on the long term say this kind of reaction is ridiculous. They are probably right about that. Yet instead of embracing what they obviously believe is an irrational sell-off as an opportunity to purchase more shares at a reduced price, they are trying to eliminate volatility by eliminating guidance. Yet there is no good reason to believe that eliminating guidance will reduce volatility in the least. It would be much more effective to eliminate quarterly earnings announcements altogether. However, no one is seriously suggesting we do that.

Announcement date volatility was a particularly frustrating problem for individual investors prior to October 2000. Back then corporations routinely excluded individual investors from conference calls. They held these calls when they had something important to announce, such as quarterly earnings. They also often provided revenue and earnings guidance during these calls.

The SEC began hearing complaints about this kind of selective disclosure from those who were excluded from the calls. The SEC also noticed that stock prices would often rise or fall suddenly while the calls were still in progress. This was because those who were privy to the material information being disclosed were executing trades or tipping off favored clients before the rest of the market became aware of the news.

In order to create a more level playing field, the SEC promulgated Regulation Fair Disclosure (or Reg FD), which mandated that corporations release nonpublic material information in a fair and timely manner. This information must now be disclosed simultaneously to everyone. Companies can no longer release material information only to a select group of analysts and investors. Most corporations now broadcast their conference calls over the Web. Today, anyone can listen to these calls while they are still in progress. Every investor can now get access to the same information at the same time as the professionals. You do not even have to be a shareholder of the company to listen in on these calls. Although corporations are still permitted to meet with analysts and institutional investors on a one-on-one basis, they are prohibited from saying anything that could be considered material and nonpublic. If they do so inadvertently, they must make a public announcement of that same information and file this announcement with the SEC within twenty-four hours.

Even though Reg FD gives all investors access to material information at the same time, stock prices still react violently to earnings announcements. That is not likely to change if guidance is eliminated. Furthermore, if management stops providing guidance, there is a good chance that some analysts will stop covering the stock. This may not be a problem for large companies with a wide following, such as Coca-Cola, but analyst coverage is not something a small company can take for granted. For a small-cap company, reduced coverage can reduce interest in the stock, which can increase the company's cost of capital. And what about those analysts who continue to cover the stock after management ends guidance? They are not going to stop estimating earnings. That is a critical part of their job. Just imagine how clients would react if an analyst produced a research report that contained no earnings projections. Analysts make earnings estimates because clients demand the information. But if corporations stop providing guidance, analysts' estimates are more likely to be wrong. Many investors already complain that the disparity between actual earnings and the consensus estimate produced by analysts is much too large. Without guidance, it will become larger.

Furthermore, ending guidance will not stop managers from forming their own expectations for internal purposes. All well-run companies must create short-run budgets. They must estimate revenues and expenses for the coming weeks, months, and quarters. Even if they stop providing guidance to investors, they will still make earnings and cash flow projections for themselves. The only difference is they will not tell the rest of us what they expect. This does not sound like a particularly good idea. Less information being released to the market creates greater uncertainty; and greater uncertainty means more risk. Investors may still be willing to buy the shares of a company that no longer provides guidance, but only at a lower price. The inevitable result for the corporation is a higher cost of capital.

A Look at the Evidence

You may think the opinions expressed here are nothing but conjecture. Think again. There is plenty of empirical evidence suggesting that eliminating earnings guidance is a bad idea. A University of Washington study examined ninety-six companies that formally announced an end to quarterly earnings guidance between 2000 and 2006.[2] The findings should make every concerned investor sit up and take notice. Eliminating earnings guidance results in a statistically significant loss of shareholder wealth.

Critics sometimes argue that what is statistically significant may not be economically meaningful. So here is another way to look at the results: on average, a company with a $10 billion market capitalization would experience approximately a $480 million loss in value over a three-day period when management simply announces that quarterly earnings guidance will no longer be provided. That should be economically meaningful enough to get anybody's attention!

Furthermore, this announcement date sell-off is not just a one-shot deal. It turns out that companies ending guidance continue to do worse than their benchmarks over the next year as well.[3] In addition, analysts' earnings estimates for these companies become less accurate. As conjectured, it is indeed true that the disparity between actual earnings and the consensus estimate gets larger for companies that stop providing guidance.

The authors of the study believe that eliminating earnings guidance signals to investors that management is less optimistic about future cash flows. It is no coincidence that many of the companies that decided to eliminate guidance were already having trouble meeting the consensus estimates in previous quarters. These companies have somehow convinced themselves that it is better to keep quiet about earnings expectations than it is to be quantitatively candid about troubles ahead.

A second study out of New York University and the University of Florida examined the effects of stopping and resuming earnings guidance.[4] The authors of this study identified 222 companies that ended guidance between 2002 and 2005, 26 of which formally announced an end to earnings guidance and 196 that simply stopped providing guidance without making an announcement. These companies were having a particularly difficult time meeting or beating earnings estimates. They stopped providing guidance because business was not going so well, not because they genuinely believed that ending guidance was good for shareholders. Interestingly, the authors also found that many of the companies actually resumed the practice of providing earnings guidance once business conditions improved.

Furthermore, the authors of this study found that analyst coverage does indeed decrease for guidance stoppers, which may explain why many companies are reluctant to give up the practice despite growing pressure from organizations such as the U.S. Chamber of Commerce.[5] They also found that analysts' earnings estimates become less accurate when guidance is not provided. And contrary to popular belief, the authors found that companies that end guidance do not provide other kinds of information. Basically, less guidance simply means less information—period. Perhaps most troubling, they found no evidence that guidance stoppers are any more likely to take actions that enhance long-term value. For example, they do not increase capital expenditures or investments in research and development. The authors concluded, "We cannot endorse the frequently voiced recommendation to firms to cease providing quarterly guidance."[6] Based on rigorous and thorough research, it is difficult to find anything good to say about ending earnings guidance.

No Guidance at Berkshire

Warren Buffett is an extremely successful investor who has a stellar and well-deserved reputation for doing what is best for shareholders. As a result, when he takes a strong position on an issue, the rest of the investment community tends to fall in line. No one wants to be seen opposing Buffett. Because Buffett hates earnings guidance, it has become fashionable for others in the investment industry to speak out against it, too.

Berkshire Hathaway does not provide guidance, and Berkshire shareholders seem perfectly fine with this arrangement. After all, why insist on guidance when you have Warren Buffett running your company? Berkshire shareholders can live without guidance because they trust Buffett. Buffett has also convinced some of the publicly traded companies in Berkshire's portfolio to stop giving guidance. Direct investors in these companies are also comfortable living without guidance. They feel a sense of security owning the same stocks that Berkshire owns. But not every company has Warren Buffett in the corner office or the boardroom. Not every company benefits from Buffett's insight and oversight. Just because a no-guidance policy works well at Berkshire and certain companies Berkshire owns does not make it right for every corporation.

To really appreciate how much clout Buffett carries, compare AT&T to Coca-Cola. When AT&T said on January 23, 2003, after the market closed, that it was putting an end to earnings guidance, the stock price plunged. The following day it closed down 19 percent, or $4.83 per share. But when Coca-Cola made the same announcement just a month earlier, the stock held up fairly well. Over the course of the next two trading days Coca-Cola lost only about 2 percent, or 93 cents per share. Of course, there were many important differences between these two companies at the time, any one of which could have explained the dramatically different stock-price reactions. Yet one key difference cannot be overlooked. Buffett sat on Coca-Cola's board when it announced an end to earnings guidance. AT&T, however, did not have Buffett aboard to provide the same level of assurance to its shareholders.

The empirical evidence is clear. Encouraging corporations to stop providing earnings guidance is not a particularly good idea. When guidance is eliminated, shareholders suffer a significant loss in wealth, fewer analysts continue to cover the company, and consensus earnings estimates become less accurate. Furthermore, there is nothing to suggest that companies that end guidance provide additional information about long-term strategic plans, and there is no evidence that they increase investments that maximize long-term value. While larger companies with widespread ownership that enjoy a lot of coverage may be able to get away with stopping guidance, smaller companies are likely to pay a heavy price if they end the practice.

Perhaps most worrisome is that there are those who think it is not enough to simply encourage companies to end guidance. They want to see an outright regulatory ban. But in an era still recovering from corporate scandals, regulators should be doing all they can to urge corporations to disclose more information, not less. Banning guidance through regulatory channels would be as wrongheaded as mandating it. The decision to provide or not provide guidance should be left to management. Even though the empirical evidence suggests shareholders are better served receiving guidance, there may be times when management decides that keeping mum is the best strategy. For example, they may legitimately fear that providing specific earnings guidance might tip off competitors. Of course, if investors do not agree with management's decision, they will let them know by selling the stock and bidding down the price. Regulation that bans guidance—or mandates it—will harm shareholders more than it will help them.

KEY TAKEAWAYS: CHAPTER 10

- Buffett believes guidance encourages short-term thinking and causes executives to manage earnings expectations rather than the business. But guidance is not what causes investors to form expectations. The blame for that goes to the SEC, which requires corporations to report financial results every quarter. Even if companies stop providing guidance, investors will continue to form quarterly earnings expectations. *Avoid investing in companies that refuse to provide earnings guidance, especially if they also fail to provide other kinds of specific information that can help investors understand how the business is likely to do in future periods.*

- Much of the opposition to guidance is rooted in the stock-price volatility that often accompanies a company's earnings announcement. Share prices can fluctuate wildly even if per-share earnings miss the consensus estimate by just a penny or two. *If you really believe that an earnings-related sell-off is unjustified, you should welcome it as an opportunity to buy more shares at a lower price.*

- Researchers report a statistically and economically significant loss in shareholder wealth when guidance is eliminated. Also, the end of guidance results in less coverage by analysts and less accurate earning estimates. Furthermore, there is no evidence that guidance stoppers take steps to enhance long-term shareholder value. *If you own stock in a company that you suspect is about to end guidance, consider selling it quickly. Do not buy it back until you are convinced that business conditions are on the mend.*

- Some companies suffer a severe sell-off when they end guidance. Others do not experience much of a reaction at all. The difference is sometimes due to management's credibility. *Management credibility is especially critical if you are investing for the long term. All companies will experience rough patches, but those with reputable managers at the helm are more likely to weather slowdowns even if they end earnings guidance or take other actions that do not necessarily serve the best interests of investors in the short run.*

Conclusion

Warren Buffett is a legend in his own time. He is arguably the greatest investor who ever lived. He is perhaps the most written about as well. A recent search for "Warren Buffett" in the "books" category of Amazon.com turned up 2,897 results. At least one hundred of them had the word "Buffett" in the title. The publication of this book adds to that list.

Investors are clearly fascinated with Buffett. Much of the adulation is a direct result of his tremendous success and wealth. He is, after all, one of the richest men in the entire world. Not long ago, he agreed to give the bulk of his wealth to a foundation run by Bill Gates, the founder of Microsoft and a Berkshire director who, like Buffett, is one of the world's richest individuals. But it is not just the thickness of Buffett's wallet or his incredible generosity that makes him the focus of so much attention. Investors are just as intrigued by his personality. Despite his tremendous wealth and intelligence, he comes across as an ordinary Joe. People love his extraordinary ability to exercise common sense, his self-deprecating humor, and his almost complete lack of ego. Buffett is a cross between Albert Einstein and Andy Griffith's Sheriff Taylor from the 1960s television series. You can't help but admire him, respect him, and like him a whole hell of a lot. First, you want to tap his brain on just about any subject you can think of. Then, you would like to sit on his front porch and share a slice of Aunt Bee's apple pie.

Perhaps the most intriguing thing about Warren Buffett is that he cannot easily be pigeonholed. In fact, trying to classify Buffett's investment strategies is a mistake frequently made by many writers and researchers. Investment professionals as well love to put their colleagues into little boxes, seal the boxes, and attach neatly typed labels on them. They say things like, "This guy is a value investor." Or, "That guy is a growth investor." However, there is no convenient label for Buffett. Buffett is a value investor who also buys growth stocks. Buffett is a buy-and-hold investor who also trades. Buffett prefers to invest in large-cap companies, but he also goes after small- and midcap companies. Buffett buys American companies and stocks, but he recently began purchasing foreign businesses. Buffett is best known as a buyer of individual stocks and entire companies, but he also buys fixed-income securities such as bonds. Indeed, Buffett even dabbles in currencies, commodities, and derivatives. It really is impossible to put Buffett into an investment box. There are no appropriate investment labels for him. Once you think you have figured out his style, he changes it.

Furthermore, many Buffett-watchers believe he is solid as a rock. In other words, they think he follows a small set of principles and never strays from them. They believe he has become successful by simply implementing the same basic strategies over and over again. They also like to believe that anyone can be a tremendously successful investor just by learning some of Buffett's favorite tricks and doing what he has done in the past.

If only things were that simple. Buffett's investment style is not rock solid. If anything, it is more like molten lava. This is because he is constantly changing and refining his strategies. Buffett knows full well that no investor can expect to become tremendously successful by simply repeating the same formulaic steps over and over again. To be truly successful, investors must be willing to mold their styles and strategies as conditions warrant. Buffett has always been a student of the markets. He did not stop learning simply because he graduated from business school. Buffett's education never came to an end, and neither should yours.

Yet despite his willingness to change and adapt to his surroundings, there are three things about Buffett that are constant. First, he clearly loves the insurance business. Buffett's personal wealth is the direct result of just one stock—Berkshire Hathaway—and Berkshire's success is largely due to just one industry—insurance. By steering Berkshire into the insurance business, Buffett was able to get his hands on a tremendous amount of float. He realized long ago that Berkshire could earn a fortune by taking the premiums received from selling insurance policies and investing them at rates of return that were high enough to pay future claims and still have plenty left over for shareholders.

The second thing about Buffett that has remained constant throughout his career is the importance he places on good-quality management. Based on his writings, one might even get the impression that little else matters. Good management is indeed very important for creating long-term value. This is consistent with finance theory, which says a poorly managed company will be worth more if another management team gains control and does a better job of investing the assets and operating the business. This is one reason often cited for hostile takeovers. Buffett, however, is not at all fond of hostile takeovers. He has absolutely no interest in going after poorly managed companies because he has no interest in managing them himself. Instead, he invites business principals of well-run companies to contact him directly if they are willing to sell to Berkshire. But he does not want these managers to retire and go away after the sale. Buffett is interested only in buying good companies with good managers who are willing to stay on and keep running the show.

Buffett is also big on ethics. In particular, he wants all his managers to understand that shareholders come first. He has no problem with good managers making lots of money as long as the shareholders become wealthy too, but he is disgusted by the excess of greed witnessed in many corporations in recent years. Buffett has seen too many CEOs loaded up with too many stock options and other incentives that make it almost impossible for them not to become wealthy, even if the company and the stock do not do particularly well. He also has seen too many companies resort to accounting gimmicks and other manipulations, such as share repurchases, that make little economic sense but boost the stock price—at least long enough to enrich the executives who exercise their options and quickly sell their shares. In general, Buffett has seen too many executives benefit personally at the expense of their own shareholders.

Third, Buffett relies heavily on a discounted cash flow (DCF) analysis to find stocks and companies that can be purchased for less than intrinsic value. Finance theory tells us that the value of any asset is simply equal to the present value of all the future cash flows the asset is expected to generate. Although Buffett is not always fond of esoteric finance theories and frequently disagrees with members of the academic community, DCF analysis is one topic that Buffett and the academics agree on wholeheartedly. While ordinary investors are sometimes intimidated by the DCF methodology, it is not nearly as complicated as it appears. By studying some Wall Street research reports and working through a few spreadsheets, you can acquire the skills and confidence to employ the methodology to identify stocks that are selling for less than they are worth.

Yet it is important to stress that DCF analysis is used to find *undervalued* stocks—not value stocks. This is an often unappreciated distinction. An undervalued stock is a stock that can be purchased for less than its intrinsic value. A value stock is simply a stock that has low price multiples. While there is ample evidence that value stocks outperform growth stocks (i.e., stocks with high price multiples) over long investment horizons, value stocks are not always undervalued and growth stocks are not always overvalued. Buffett relies on DCF analysis to identify undervalued stocks. It is always best to buy stocks that are selling for less than they are worth. However, there is a catch with this kind of thinking. When you conclude that a stock is undervalued, you are presuming that you are correct in your analysis and that everyone else in the market is wrong. After all, if everyone agreed that the stock was truly undervalued, they would have already started buying it and bid its price up to fair value.

This brings us to another important issue. While Buffett agrees with the academics on the theoretical value of DCF analysis, he disagrees with them on a number of other points. For example, many academics (and a good number of practitioners) strongly believe that markets are efficient, meaning that stock prices accurately reflect their true values. As a result, they do not believe it is possible to consistently outperform the market indexes over long periods of time by picking stocks on a selective basis. While they admit that superior investors like Buffett do in fact exist, they simply dismiss them out of hand by calling them anomalies. Buffett, however, does not subscribe to modern portfolio theory and the efficient markets hypothesis. He believes there are so many of these so-called anomalies that an intelligent investor must question the validity of modern portfolio theory. Buffett believes that smart investors who do their homework, make a habit of purchasing only undervalued stocks, and hold on to them for the long term can and often do beat the market averages. While many investors idolize Buffett and hold him up as evidence that markets are not efficient, Buffett himself prefers to cite Walter Schloss, an investment guru who consistently beat the market over a forty-seven-year career.

Diversification is another academic favorite. However, Buffett's message on diversification is mixed. The academics say everyone should hold an extensively diversified portfolio. They frequently recommend investing in mutual funds or exchange traded funds that track broad-based indexes. According to the academics, diversification will ensure that investors get the highest expected return for any given level of risk. However, diversification locks investors into the market rate of return. Those that hold a broadly diversified portfolio have no hope of beating the market.

Until relatively recently, Berkshire's portfolio was extremely concentrated. These days, however, Berkshire owns more than seventy subsidiary companies, dozens of publicly traded stocks, and all kinds of fixed-income securities. Berkshire is more diversified today than at any other time in its history. Of course, to a large extent, it had no choice in the matter. Berkshire has grown so large and has so much money to invest, it can't help but diversify. Yet even today the company is less diversified than what finance theory dictates. Furthermore, Berkshire has huge positions in a relatively small number of companies and much smaller investments in all the others. Nonetheless, under Buffett's direction, Berkshire has gone from a position of extreme concentration to one that leans toward greater diversification. Buffett is also recommending greater diversification to others. He says that the vast majority of ordinary investors should extensively diversify.

However, he also argues that just a half dozen stocks provide sufficient diversification for those investors who know what they are doing and really understand how to evaluate businesses.

To reiterate, the three things that can be said for sure about Buffett are that he has a hankering for the insurance business, he puts a lot of weight on the quality of management, and he likes to buy stocks and companies that can be had for less than intrinsic value as determined by a discounted cash flow model. We can also conclude that he does not think much of modern portfolio theory, and although he favors a more concentrated approach for himself, he believes that most investors should extensively diversify.

We have also learned a number of other useful things. For example, we learned that academic research has shown that value stocks beat growth stocks over the long term, but that growth stocks are a better bet for investors with shorter horizons. We learned that small-cap stocks do better than large-cap stocks over the long term. Furthermore, we learned that momentum investing actually works. In particular, growth stocks that have strong price and earnings momentum do better than other stocks over investment horizons of about six to eighteen months. Although many investors frown on momentum-based strategies, research studies show that using momentum is a perfectly legitimate and profitable way to invest.

However, momentum investing is not for everyone. Although momentum investing is not the same as day trading, it does require considerably more turnover than a simple buy-and-hold investment strategy. As a result, momentum investors incur greater transactions costs than long-term value investors. These days, however, trading costs can be kept to a minimum thanks to online brokerage firms. Yet brokerage commissions are not the only cost to worry about. Taxes are another. Buy-and-hold investors do not have to pay much attention to taxes. After all, if you do not sell, you do not realize gains. And if you do not realize gains, you do not have to worry about paying taxes on those gains. Momentum investors, however, realize their gains quite frequently. The tax man hates buy-and-hold investors, but he loves momentum investors.

We also learned that Warren Buffett makes use of certain strategies that most ordinary investors are in no position to employ. For example, on Berkshire's behalf, he frequently acquires entire companies. Yet even when he just buys some shares in a publicly traded company, Berkshire usually ends up becoming one of the largest shareholders on record. Whether Buffett chooses to exercise it or not, he quickly puts himself into a position of significant influence. Indeed, he has sat on more than twenty corporate boards. At one time he even assumed the position of CEO at Salomon Inc. Although he does not like to do so, he has also agitated for the replacement of underperforming managers. In any case, it is certainly fair to say that Buffett is a buyer of businesses rather than a buyer of stocks. Buying stocks, however, is the most that ordinary investors can hope to do. This is because they cannot take a large enough position in any one company to exert the kind of influence Buffett regularly enjoys. Simply said, ordinary investors cannot do many of the things that have made Berkshire and Buffett so successful.

PIPEs (private investments in public equity) provide another excellent example of what Buffett does that ordinary investors cannot do. PIPEs have allowed Berkshire to garner large positions in publicly traded companies on a favorable basis. Publicly traded companies sometimes use PIPEs to gain access to large amounts of capital quickly without having to register securities with the SEC. By using PIPEs, they also minimize underwriting fees. A

PIPE typically begins life as a convertible security that pays the purchaser a stream of interest or dividends. At some point in the future, however, this security can be converted into common stock, giving the investor an equity interest in the issuing company that could be significant. If properly structured and fully disclosed, there is nothing underhanded about PIPEs. Nonetheless, they do provide yet another example of how Buffett and Berkshire sometimes implement strategies that are not at the disposal of ordinary investors. If you find the idea of investing via PIPEs intriguing, consider buying shares of Berkshire or investing in a hedge fund that regularly exploits this strategy.

Perhaps some readers were surprised to learn from this book that not all of Buffett's investments have been resounding successes. Indeed, we examined a few of Berkshire's troubled investments. Interestingly, however, we also learned that Buffett has a rather incredible knack for turning lemons into lemonade. Yet doing so often required a tremendous amount of patience. For example, Berkshire purchased both General Re and NetJets in 1998, but it was not until 2006 that these companies began making good money. Soon after buying General Re, Buffett discovered all kinds of problems, including accounting irregularities, insurance policies that had been underpriced, and rather significant derivatives-related losses. NetJets incurred tremendous costs as it tried to break into the European market. Once it started making money in Europe, things soured in the United States. However, Buffett never gave up on these companies. He continued to believe they would eventually succeed and make important contributions to Berkshire's profitability. His focus on the long term has allowed him to stick with these companies through thick and thin. The point is that long-term investing sometimes requires a tremendous amount of patience. If you have no reason to believe a company will go under, as long as the management team is competent it can often pay to sit tight and wait.

We also learned about the importance of good corporate governance and succession planning. Berkshire had a rather poor record in this area for many years. Of course, most investors did not care. After all, investors do not typically complain about governance and succession when the stock is doing well. However, in recent years many investors learned the hard way why these issues are important. Failures at Tyco, Enron, WorldCom, Adelphia, and about a dozen other notable companies occurred largely because of poor governance practices.

No one doubts that Warren Buffett is an outstanding CEO. He also ranks among the most ethical CEOs ever. Unfortunately, not all companies have the good fortune of having someone like Buffett at the helm. And as good as Buffett is, even he is not immortal. The day will come when Buffett will no longer be able to lead Berkshire. It is precisely for these reasons that governance and succession planning matter. Shareholders have to be able to rely on a board of directors that can keep the CEO from riding roughshod. They also have to feel secure knowing that plans are in place to keep the company going if something unfortunate were to happen to the head honcho. Thanks largely to new NYSE requirements, listed companies can no longer turn a deaf ear to these issues. Yet some companies do a better job than others. Furthermore, many companies whose shares trade over-the-counter do not pay much attention to governance and succession. Long-term investors learned a very expensive lesson in recent years when some of the more popular companies blew up, in part due to poor governance practices. Before sinking your money into any company, make sure it is properly governed.

Stock options have also captured the attention of investors in recent years. Contrary to popular opinion, Buffett does not oppose the use of options. Indeed, he believes options are a useful tool for rewarding corporate executives. He even predicts that his successor at Berkshire will receive a large portion of his compensation from options. However, Buffett is strongly opposed to the abuse of options. He thinks directors need to do a much better job of structuring options in a way that truly rewards executives for adding value and not just for showing up during a bull market. He also believes options are not free. Buffett is one of the most vocal advocates for requiring the expensing of stock options when they are granted on corporate income statements. Yet the fact remains that there really is no expense to an option until it is actually exercised. Tax accounting recognizes this simple fact, but financial accounting does not. As a result, for financial accounting purposes, options are valued when they are granted and expensed when they vest. But for tax accounting purposes, options are expensed only when they are exercised. Expensing options before they are exercised is as misleading as not expensing them at all. Furthermore, the different accounting and tax treatments add to investors' confusion. In any case, investors should be wary about investing in a company if the quarterly stock option expense amounts to much more than just a few pennies per share.

Some readers may have been at least a little surprised to learn how strongly Buffett has opposed efforts to reduce taxes. For example, Buffett favors the estate tax. He believes everyone should have to earn his or her own keep, and he has long made it clear that his heirs can expect to receive very little from him when he passes on. Those like Buffett fear that, in the absence of high estate taxes, individuals who have amassed large amounts of wealth would simply pass it on to their heirs, creating generations of good-for-nothing spoiled brats and providing no overall benefit to society. Yet the fact is that those who are faced with a substantial estate tax can plan ahead and mitigate this burden either by buying estate tax insurance (perhaps from one of Berkshire's companies) or by exploiting certain tax loopholes. The biggest loophole allows the wealthy to donate money to a foundation before passing on. Indeed, this is exactly what Buffett is doing. While he should be applauded for his extraordinary generosity, his decision to give his money away effectively keeps it out of the government's hands.

Buffett also favors higher taxes on investment income. Indeed, he actively petitioned against efforts to eliminate personal taxes on dividends, even though dividends are paid to shareholders only after corporations have paid their own taxes. In other words, the situation results in double taxation. Nonetheless, Buffett believes that reducing taxes on investment income benefits only those who are wealthy enough to invest. Yet the fact is that lower tax rates benefit everyone by stimulating economic growth and increasing federal tax receipts. Stronger economic growth means better job opportunities for all members of society. Taxing the investment class at higher rates is likely to do more harm than good. When politicians start chattering about raising taxes on the rich, it's usually a good time to start taking money out of the market. When they start talking about reducing tax rates, you should consider buying more stocks.

Finally, we learned that Buffett wants to see corporations put an end to earnings guidance. He believes providing guidance encourages short-term thinking on the part of investors and corporate managers. Buffett is not the only one who feels this way. Several commentators and organizations have jumped on this bandwagon. However, the belief that guidance is responsible for short-term thinking is a misconception. No one argues that running a corporation with the long term in mind is not the superior approach, but it is wrong to believe that guidance causes short-term thinking. No doubt, investors do focus on quarterly earnings numbers, but not because corporations dispense guidance. Investors pay attention to quarterly results for only one reason—the SEC requires corporations to report results on a quarterly basis. It is because of this SEC requirement that investors form quarterly expectations. If the SEC told corporations to report results on a monthly basis, investors would form monthly expectations. This has nothing to do with guidance. Eliminating guidance will in no way stop investors from forming expectations.

Furthermore, guidance provides valuable information. At least two research studies prove that earnings estimates become less accurate when guidance is not provided. In an era in which regulators are trying to promote more disclosure, it makes no sense to encourage corporations to stop giving guidance.

There are a number of companies that have never provided guidance. This does not mean that investors should avoid buying them. Berkshire Hathaway has never provided guidance, yet it has proven to be one of the best long-term investments on the market. However, red flags should be raised when a company that previously provided guidance suddenly decides to eliminate it.

As *Forbes* magazine makes clear every year, there are plenty of billionaires in the world. Yet few have reached the upper echelon of this prestigious list by investing. Most, such as Microsoft founder Bill Gates, owe their fortunes to just one company. Warren Buffett, on the other hand, is a true investor. Even though his fortune is also due to just one company, that company, Berkshire Hathaway, is unique. Indeed, Berkshire is really an investment company. Buffett built Berkshire by reinvesting insurance-related cash flows into other businesses. He made himself rich in the process. More important, however, he made his shareholders rich as well. Perhaps no other single individual has created more millionaires. Based on the evidence, it is certainly fair to conclude that Warren Buffett is one of the greatest investors—if not *the* greatest investor—of all time.

Afterword

Soon after the initial publication of this book, global financial markets were shaken to the core. What started as an economic slowdown in the United States soon spread into a worldwide recession. The troubles all began when the air started coming out of the housing bubble. As housing prices plunged, securities backed by mortgages—especially subprime mortgages—lost most of their value. Investors started referring to them as toxic waste. Because these mortgages had been securitized and sold off in the secondary markets, institutions around the world found themselves holding paper that suddenly had little or no value.

It wasn't long before some of America's oldest and best known companies either went out of business or disappeared as independent entities. What remained of Bear Stearns, Lehman Brothers, and Merrill Lynch was absorbed by JPMorgan Chase, Barclay's, and Bank of America, respectively. A number of other finance companies, including Fannie Mae, Freddie Mac, and American International Group, collapsed and were nationalized. Not too long ago these stocks were prized for safety and income. They were almost always found as core holdings in most diversified portfolios. In fact, AIG was considered such a blue chip stock that Dow Jones even added it to its prestigious Industrial Average in 2004.

As the economic slowdown spread, troubles in the corporate

sector extended well beyond the finance companies. The CEOs of America's once-prized automobile industry went to Congress begging for help. General Motors, Ford, and Chrysler were suddenly shadows of their former great selves. Even plunging gasoline prices were not enough to bring customers back into the showrooms.

Investors reacted to all this bad news as they so often do—by dumping stocks. They sold everything they could—the good with the bad. Some sold out of fear. Others were forced to sell to meet margin calls. Even sophisticated institutional investors such as hedge funds and mutual funds began dumping their holding to meet redemptions. A five-year-long bull market quickly melted into one of the most severe bear markets since the Great Depression.

Into the fray walked Warren Buffett. The man who not too long ago complained that he could not find anything worth buying (see chapter 5) suddenly saw opportunity. The man who said, "Be fearful when others are greedy, and be greedy when others are fearful," made major investments in Goldman Sachs and General Electric. Yet he did not simply buy the common shares. Instead, as he so often does, he cut special deals for his Berkshire Hathaway shareholders. He bought preferred stock paying a 10 percent dividend, and he also got warrants to buy the common stock at prices that were already in the money. As explained in chapter 4, this use of PIPEs (private investment in public equity) is Buffett's modus operandi.

Buffett is a buy-and-hold investor who says his favorite holding period is "forever." He welcomes bear markets as long-term buying opportunities. However, the severity of the 2008 bear market taught investors that Buffett's way is not always the best way to invest. Those who followed a long-term buy-and-hold strategy with stocks like Bear Stearns, Lehman Brothers, Merrill

Lynch, Fannie Mae, Freddie Mac, AIG, GM, and Ford got crushed. Indeed, many stocks and most major market indexes fell to levels not seen for a decade or longer. There is no doubt investors would have been better served selling their holdings long before the meltdown began. As chapter 4 explains, this is why you should "Never Marry a Stock."

As far as many Berkshire Hathaway shareholders are concerned, Warren Buffett is the closest thing to God, so they do not like to question his decisions. This became extremely clear at the 2008 shareholders' meeting. Just weeks before the meeting, Joseph Brandon, CEO of General Re unexpectedly resigned. Rumor had it that federal prosecutors pressured Buffett to let Brandon go because they believed he was somehow involved in a scheme that got four former General Re and one former AIG executive convicted for fraud. In fact, Brandon was named as an unindicted coconspirator in that case. Buffett has frequently praised Brandon in his annual letters to shareholders—including the one released before the 2008 meeting. Brandon was even believed to be on the short list of possible Buffett successors. However, Buffett made no comment at the shareholders' meeting about Brandon's sudden resignation. More amazingly, not one shareholder who was lucky enough to get to a microphone asked about it. Instead, shareholders asked Buffett questions like, "What should I do with the rest of my life?"

Of course, Buffett is not God, but his long-term investment track record is certainly superb. Yet even Buffett makes mistakes. In hindsight, for example, Berkshire's $5 billion investment in Goldman Sachs and its $3 billion investment in General Electric were made too soon. Although Berkshire received warrants that were already in the money at the time, just a few months after those deals were struck both stocks were selling for only half their respective exercise prices. Of course, as Buffett makes perfectly clear, he does not care how any of his investments fare over the short run. He is interested only in how well they perform over the long run. Buffett is convinced that as the economy recovers and growth resumes, both Goldman Sachs and General Electric will thrive. He may be right about that. However, with Berkshire's shares down more than 40 percent at one point in 2008, it is certainly fair to say that "Even Buffett Isn't Perfect."

Acknowledgments

In September 2006, while being driven to a television studio to do an interview about the economy, I received an e-mail on my BlackBerry from Jeffrey Krames, a man I had never heard of before. The e-mail invited me to contact him to discuss writing a book. At first, I thought it was spam. Fortunately, I followed up on Jeffrey's invitation the next day. Before I knew what happened, I was immersed in a year-long endeavor. I thank Jeffrey and his able editorial assistant Courtney Young for encouraging me and guiding me throughout the process of writing this book.

I am grateful to so many of my current and former colleagues at Forbes Inc., especially to the members of the Forbes family. I thank Wally, Tim, and Steve, who decided in 1997 to hire an unknown and relatively young finance professor to be the new editor of the *Forbes Special Situation Survey*, an investment newsletter started in 1954 by their late brother and father, Malcolm. The Forbes family has given me many wonderful opportunities during the past decade. Working with them has been a tremendous pleasure. I also thank Leonard Yablon, who continues to keep tabs on me to this day, making sure I am always thinking about the markets.

All these wonderful opportunities at Forbes have come with serious responsibilities. Publishing two monthly investment newsletters that are highly ranked by the *Hulbert Financial Digest,* producing a biweekly Internet video program, and providing regular commentary on the economy and markets for numerous radio and television stations are more than enough to keep me busy. It would have been impossible to do all this, and write a book too, without the extraordinary assistance I receive each and every day from our two equity analysts, Taesik Yoon and Samuel Ro. I couldn't ask for better employees.

Of course, I must mention the wonderful teachers who inspired me many years ago at Lower Merion High School, Villanova University, and Virginia Tech. I am especially grateful to Robert Hansen, Art Keown, and John Pinkerton. As members of my dissertation committee, they proved I was capable of working much harder than I ever thought was possible.

Finally, but most important, I am extremely grateful to my entire family. Warren Buffett says he is lucky to have been born in America. I am lucky that my father and mother saw fit to immigrate to America when my sister, Kayane, and I were very young. I am also lucky that my mother got me interested in investing when I was just a teenager. I owe special thanks to my wonderful wife and our three lovely daughters. Nooné not only served as my initial reviewer; she also assumed many of my responsibilities at home so I could devote more time to my writing. Lori, Luciné, and Lily demonstrated tremendous patience and understanding throughout the process. I worked late on too many occasions and cheated them out of too much time with their dad. Hey, kids, it's finally over! Let's go play some soccer.

Notes

Introduction

1. Roger G. Ibbotson and Rex A. Sinquefield, *Stocks, Bonds, Bills, and Inflation (SBBI) Yearbook* (Chicago: Ibbotson Associates, 2006), p. 31.

1. The *New* Diversified Buffett?

1. Berkshire Hathaway Inc., chairman's letter to shareholders, 1993.
2. Leslie P. Norton, "Chairman Buffett's Maxims," *Barron's*, May 13, 1996, p. 45.
3. An exchange traded fund is similar to a mutual fund in the sense that it is just a basket of stocks. However, its price fluctuates continuously and shares can be purchased and sold throughout the day. A mutual fund is priced just once a day and all transactions are completed at that price. Exchange traded funds also offer certain tax advantages over mutual funds.
4. Derived from Berkshire Hathaway's Web site and its Form 13F filings with the Securities and Exchange Commission.
5. Forbes.com Web site.
6. Gary Brinson, Randolph Hood, and Gilbert Beebower, "Determinants of Portfolio Performance," *Financial Analysts Journal,* vol. 42, no. 4 (July/Aug. 1986), pp. 39–44.
7. James Altucher, *Trade Like Warren Buffett* (Hoboken, N.J.: John Wiley & Sons, Inc., 2005), p. 4.
8. Berkshire Hathaway Inc., *2005 Annual Report,* p. 6.
9. Jeremy J. Siegel, *Stocks for the Long Run* (Chicago: Richard D. Irwin, 1994), p. 31.

2. The Undervalued Buffett

1. Liz Claman, "Buffett Raw," CNBC, Dec. 2006.
2. Berkshire Hathaway Inc., *2006 Annual Report,* p. 22.
3. Ibid.
4. Investors sometimes wonder why Berkshire's shares sell for so high a price. It is simply because Buffett refuses to split the stock. He believes stock splits have no economic justification. Buffett folklore has it that he sometimes sends birthday greetings to friends wishing they live until he splits the stock.
5. Berkshire Hathaway Inc., *2005 Annual Report,* p. 77.

3. Value for the Long Run, Growth for the Short

1. Eugene F. Fama and Kenneth R. French, "The Cross-Section of Expected Stock Returns," *Journal of Finance,* vol. 47, no. 2 (June 1992), pp. 427–465.
2. Eugene F. Fama and Kenneth R. French, "Value Versus Growth: The International Evidence," *Journal of Finance,* vol. 53, no. 6 (Dec. 1998), pp. 1975–1999.
3. Narasimhan Jegadeesh and Sheridan Titman, "Returns to Buying Winners and Selling Losers: Implications for Stock Market Efficiency," *Journal of Finance,* vol. 48, no. 1 (Mar. 1993), pp. 65–91.
4. Louis K.C. Chan, Narasimhan Jegadeesh, and Josef Lakonishok, "Momentum Strategies," *Journal of Finance,* vol. 51, no. 5 (Dec. 1996), pp. 1681–1713.

4. Never Marry a Stock

1. Berkshire Hathaway Inc., *2005 Annual Report,* p. 6.
2. Kenneth L. Fisher, "Philip A. Fisher, 1907–2004," Forbes.com, Apr. 26, 2004.
3. "Overview: Private Investment in Public Equity ("PIPES"), A Friedland Capital White Paper," www.friedlandworldwide.com, July 25, 2005.
4. Gretchen Morgenson and Jenny Anderson, "Secrets in the Pipeline," *The New York Times,* Aug. 13, 2006.
5. James Altucher, *Trade Like Warren Buffett* (Hoboken, N.J.: John Wiley & Sons, Inc., 2005), pp. 129–141.

5. What Buffett Buys

1. This statement has appeared every year since 1998 in the "Acquisition Criteria" section of Berkshire Hathaway's annual reports. The stated range was smaller prior to 1998. And as we saw in chapter 3, Buffett is now looking to spend as much as $60 billion for a single acquisition.
2. Ibid.
3. Berkshire Hathaway Inc., *2004 Annual Report*, p. 3.
4. Berkshire Hathaway Inc., *2005 Annual Report*, p. 5.
5. Sherman Goldenberg, "News Maker '05," *RV Business*, Dec. 2005, pp. 36–39.
6. Berkshire Hathaway Inc., *2005 Annual Report*, p. 5.
7. Neal Sandler, "Buffett Tours Plant in War-scarred Tefen," *BusinessWeek* Online, Sept. 18, 2006.
8. Berkshire Hathaway Inc., *2006 Annual Report*, p. 5.
9. Ibid.
10. Ibid., p. 6.
11. Fruit of the Loom also agreed to purchase VF Corp.'s intimate apparel business for $350 million.
12. Berkshire has since liquidated its holdings of PetroChina. Buffett claims his decision to sell was based solely on valuation and had nothing to do with shareholder pressure to divest because of PetroChina's relationship with the government of Sudan, which is accused of perpetrating genocide in Darfur.

6. When "Good" Investments Go Bad

1. Berkshire Hathaway Inc., chairman's letter to shareholders, 1993.
2. For a more complete analysis of Berkshire's Salomon investment, see Carol J. Loomis and Maria Atanasov, "Warren Buffett's Wild Ride at Salomon," *Fortune*, vol. 136, no. 8 (Oct. 27, 1997), pp. 114ff.
3. Robert Lenzner, "The Secrets of Salomon," *Forbes*, Nov. 23, 1992, pp. 123ff.
4. Berkshire Hathaway Inc., *2005 Annual Report*, p. 25.
5. Berkshire Hathaway Inc., *1999 Annual Report*, p. 4.
6. Ibid.
7. Berkshire Hathaway Inc., *2000 Annual Report*, p. 10.
8. Berkshire Hathaway Inc., *2001 Annual Report*, p. 3.

9. Ibid.

10. Berkshire Hathaway Inc., *2002 Annual Report,* p. 8.

11. Ibid., p. 14.

12. Ibid., p. 15.

13. Berkshire Hathaway Inc., *2001 Annual Report,* p. 60.

14. Berkshire Hathaway Inc., *2004 Annual Report,* p. 15.

7. Governance and the Next Buffett

1. Sanjai Bhagat and Bernard Black, "The Uncertain Relationship Between Board Composition and Firm Performance," *Business Lawyer,* vol. 54 (1999), pp. 921–963.

2. Council of Institutional Investors, "Corporate Governance Policies," Feb. 2006. Available at www.cii.org.

3. Berkshire Hathaway Inc., *2004 Annual Report,* p. 23.

4. For example, see Berkshire Hathaway Inc., *2003 Annual Report,* p. 10.

5. Berkshire Hathaway Inc., "Corporate Governance Guidelines," as amended Feb. 27, 2006.

6. Berkshire Hathaway Inc., *2005 Annual Report,* p. 21.

7. Brandon has since left the company. It is believed that federal prosecutors pressured Buffett to let him go due to his alleged involvement in the AIG case discussed in Chapter 6. Brandon was never charged with any crime. Amazingly, not one shareholder inquired about Brandon's resignation at the 2008 shareholder meeting, and Buffett made no comment about it.

8. Berkshire Hathaway Inc., *2004 Annual Report,* p. 19.

9. Berkshire Hathaway Inc., *2006 Annual Report,* p. 17.

10. Ibid.

11. Ibid.

8. No Options for Buffett

1. Vahan Janjigian, "Counting on the SEC," July 26, 2006, Forbes .com/moneymasters.

2. Warren Buffett, "Stock Options and Common Sense," *The Washington Post,* Apr. 9, 2002, p. A19.

3. Burton Malkiel and William Baumol, "Stock Options Keep the Economy Afloat," *The Wall Street Journal,* Apr. 4, 2002, p. A18.

4. John Doerr and Frederick Smith, "Leave Options Alone," *The New York Times,* Apr. 5, 2002, p. 23.
5. Berkshire Hathaway Inc., *2004 Annual Report,* p. 24.
6. Ibid.

9. The Pro-Tax Buffett

1. Liberals, of course, will point to the Bush deficits. The deficits, however, are a result of increased spending, not lower tax revenues.
2. Berkshire Hathaway Inc., *2003 Annual Report,* pp. 6–7.
3. Berkshire Hathaway Inc., *2006 Annual Report,* p. 19.
4. Warren Buffett, "Dividend Voodoo," *The Washington Post,* May 20, 2003.
5. It could be argued that share buybacks are still the better choice because they leave the decision up to the investor. After all, if you don't sell your shares, you incur no tax liability.
6. Buffett, "Dividend Voodoo."
7. Milton Friedman, "278 Economists Tell Congress 'End the Death Tax Now!,'" National Taxpayers Union Foundation, www.ntu.org, May 21, 2001.
8. Pat Boone, "Super Rich Nonsense," *The Washington Times,* June 20, 2004.
9. Andrew Bary, "Death and No Taxes? What's Good for You May Be Bad for Life Insurance Companies," *Barron's,* Feb. 19, 2001.
10. Review & Outlook (Editorial), "Mr. Buffett's Tax Advice," *The Wall Street Journal,* Mar. 9, 2004.
11. Buffett is not donating this money all at once. He will give about 5 percent each year. The government will collect if Buffett dies before all the money is dispensed.

10. Give Us Guidance

1. Richard W. Leftwich, Ross L. Watts, and Jerold L. Zimmerman, "Voluntary Corporate Disclosure: The Case of Interim Reporting," *Journal of Accounting Research,* vol. 19 (1981), pp. 50–77.
2. Shuping Chen, Dawn A. Matsumoto, and Shivaram Rajgopal, "Is Silence Golden? An Empirical Analysis of Firms That Stop Giving Quarterly Earnings Guidance" (Oct. 2006). Available at SSRN: http://ssrn.com/abstract=820644.

3. Vahan Janjigian and Michael Ozanian, "Gimme Guidance," Forbes .com, Aug. 22, 2006.

4. Joel F. Houston, Baruch Itamar Lev, and Jenny Tucker, "To Guide or Not to Guide? Causes and Consequences of Stopping Quarterly Earnings Guidance" (Feb. 2007). Available at SSRN: http://ssrn .com/abstract=875184.

5. U.S. Chamber of Commerce, Commission on the Regulation of U.S. Capital Markets in the 21st Century, Report and Recommendations, Mar. 2007.

6. Houston, Lev, and Tucker, "To Guide or Not to Guide," p. 33.

Index

Page numbers in *italics* refer to figures.